My journal   Alecia Smith

AL-

EC-

IA-

Alecia Smith

-Alecia

-Smith

"Like a casket I am buried with secrets like a closet I am storage for pain. I will sing today as I am being born into today tomorrow is my home."

Diverse is my mind. Like an excel spreadsheet, I am formulating please note if you are not enhanced to calculate the stimulants to aid the use of me accurately. You may press a key and cannot reverse the methods of in- efforts to correct what was touched.

I am your mind talking to you, the thing that is ten seconds ahead of you. I am not a toy; I am your consciousness talking to you. The aspects of me are beyond today.

I may be older than you by seconds and vast to teach you beyond sight. But please remember just as your outer-body I bear the vessel to share and carry emotions.

I am the concept of night and day and all things if you recalculate me to modern-day ways to express. I am not your brain. I am a specimen of all things combined to enhance knowledge. Louder than every account. I am myself providence beyond age.

The talks of what you can master:
Master —

Complex thinking is a magnificent and creative method of how you can naturally feel the vibrations of one's crown to enhance knowledge.

The renewals of methods are an easy way to rejuvenate one's mind. Yes, but the talks to renew your mind, is in ridiculous questioning. You cannot renew anything of the mind. The mind has a method of its own.

The mind cannot be- mastered. But you can study references of how it operates. The mind takes its own- personal notes; it moves before you.

How to respond-

Tares of the rain rise. But in values shows you up. Yes, if you get wet from the rain. You will notice that you are wet. It is the same essence to see and notice that your mind as awoken before you. While you were resting, it had a plan about what is next and where I am travelling to today.

Master as the definition of one who is ready to instruct yes?
The genius in us carries a particular attitude toward life as we can be a bit much toward our exterior. So can the interior of the body. You are a shell to the mind. An organization that can be -substituted. At any given time. You have conditioned your body to this shell. But the mind as not conditioned itself to you. The very shell- you were -placed in.
You cannot master your mind.

The mind is before you. And your thoughts are in seconds of not sitting. As the very essence of the things will leave you.

-My mind.

As no rest day but my body sleeps. Yes, as I am in question to man. I say this to your attributes to contribute to the life of stating your mindset is a thing that is inaccurate to self. Why?

- The mind thinks for itself, so it is remotely impossible for you to state you must have a certain mindset when your mind is not in a settling state of life; it is forever- discovering. When you look at the mentality of things, most states it as it is your mindset again. Why?

When I look at the context of mindset, it states to me the levels of one's thoughts on the levels of how a person revolutionizes the references of having a dialect. Intelligence is an agent to the body, and the mind is self wisdom.

So I was looking at the flashing screens to approximate. Stop for a minute and look. Do you accurately remember everything from the ages of one until now? If your answer is yes, play for play, write a book on it. In detail, because that is your take on the mind. Why because the mind is a gene of itself and is made up of smart cells. To become that prodigy and a test when your changeable traits come in to play, it means you don't want to settle yes.

What I want to achieve is significant values, yes. But I must be determined by something, yes. Again life has no promises death as no waiver; it must be cashed out. You cannot stop what is meant and bound to happen, yes. So many person believe qualities are inborn when, in fact, you are- trained up to acquire those changes. Again yes, when you start developing things, you either adapt or disassociate your self from it. Key facts of life again the attitudes toward things.

I sat in meetings of my thoughts where the very notes I took drowned me as I had to learn how to swim away if I wanted to save myself from what is -called the new aged madness.

- I reduce the frequency in proximity in between others while I maintain what is called the new norms distance.
- The credits of life leave you in a transaction. Like a receipt, it hands you a piece of paper.
- Your mind is its own mastermind. How dear you question it.
- The adequates of one's mind. It is beyond you and me the adventures. It takes shine still, even if there is no sun in the sky. It takes you in winter and leaves you in fall. Your mind as its own summer-like breeze it too blows. The springs of the waves leaves you in a sitting position. Like a flood, it runs more profound and deeper.

I am making a difference by starting with myself first; upholding the integrity of others is a choice. But your dignity shouldn't be placed at cost. Who I am was always a question, but never to know who you are, is your delinquent to sell your soul effortlessly to gain fame where- the glory in giving away your rights to settle for nothing wasn't worth the cost.

If walking away from foolishness at times makes you a common denominator in life. Please continue to walk away to stand for another day because some fights are not worth standing up for.

Many things in life are of expressions, and some are of options, what sets you aside is a smile to remain humbled byways we are not the same, we are not equal. But we all have a standard of the way life is.

So when you show persons, you are better than what they think of you there is a challenge ahead to win. As time is not your friend, never fear weakness because not everyone who smiles with you is for you to achieve wealth.

You have placed me at failure as you have written books of my past as if you know my history, the side chatters define you and not me. You are not happy for me, only the pretends in your eyes. You have shown me who you are, so my quest was never to take trust lightly. I am winning, and the question is, will you be happy for me?

Da Reborn Mirror of Her:

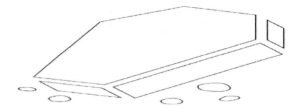

The betrayals of assurance were- taken to serve. And protect, and for you to turn around and murder my virtues. You shamed me in clothed and close me in as stain drips. My heart, you left naked. I yelled for God as he was my shield. The army of madness policed me. As I was the girl, you moved to drink water until it leaves the essence of vodka on me, your scent was my body's perfume.

I was punched in rage as I was- misinterpreted to the sound of my stain.

I was- prisoned by the ages of behind bars in my own body.

"We carry the benefits of recovery to see that at some point in our lives, we all fall from grace. As death is the killer of us, we have no escape from when it is our time."

"We see many faces to glorify the end of one's life, but often sees none when we are crying in the flesh of life."

"The pictures we take captures visions of hope. But often doesn't show your shadows in a reflection to a flash."

"My mother as given me many things that I cannot repay her for."

"As I hear the "voice" of her in my head innumerable at times, telling me how wonderful "God" is to us.

As one of her many talks was always about family and love I cry, knowing she lost out on that very essence of a mother's desire to touch. Her pain is like my beginnings to what I call genesis, as we have shared the same revelation to pain.
I am still her daughter, and she is still my mother. Pain is our madness to what causes our mental stigma. Betrayals tell no tales only shows us there is a light at the end of the tunnel. As we are still breaking in life, death is our burial to trials that fail us to testify.

"Unlock love with the thoughts and sounds of I believe in you."

"Seven, I love you! Seven times. I love you seven times".

As we are extending in a family bond, I am a queen, and my son is a king.

@Rayden-

"Legacy is not a trophy as prize sits; I am a person that feels pain."

Tick tock time is leaving us as we all exit one day in the reign of all kingdoms will one day fall.

 Things have broken us. The controversy of an introvert is I am a voice. I can speak. It just takes time to unmute me.

The sound resonates within me. The same music that opens up wounds. I am a track play me. I am- broken with a burden.

My body is a soundtrack scratch with the pain. I wear spots of a leopard beauty marks from delivery pain, play me, can you hear my sound?

--- --

"I am freed by, and still yet, I am imprisoned by. I cannot be myself as I have no needs but a feud of what was my taker. I am still at a hostage point to pain."

"Failure sees none, but accomplishments resurrect many to think they were standing with you when you were failing. I have walked alone without a purse to my hands. So, I will never ask to spend what I don't have."

- Out
- Loud
- I am

Under construction

The Eras of my own errors have ended me in an occupational hazard. To correct my madness to rewrite Alecia's occupation to spin a knob to turn her -own door in correcting my usage of English. As I am incorrect to state, I am not interspersed.

-Peace and prosperity un my mind to state all things on my mental.

"If you truly learn how to spend money, it will never purchase you because your values cost more than a dollar to spend your worth."

There is no higher start to love than loving one's self before others.

 When you can find the courage to use your worth and don't spend more than the cost, because your voice will always speak volume, positively and inspire what will need a change, then you will genuinely start living not only for self but for others.

As I am a queen set to rule, you will have no kingdom without me.
"Let your discomforts become a gift to self as uncomfortable is a pretends to win."
The lines of truth tell us we cannot discover what was already apart of existence.

Life is in the format of earth, air, wind, and water.
Elements have its part to play in life as we journey to a coarse we take on" life" as a test to reflect on what was before and after us.
Nature occurs, and space relevancy to save a life.

As the crown of life is not an ornament to be dangled, but it is a privilege to be worn on one's head. The prerogatives of a queens crown can be- taken into madness.
I am a much-needed disgrace because my mother births me in shame, so I am a sinner to mercy and sadness as testimony is grace.
My own mother's pain tells a story; that story has frequently shown her crying for outer and inner freedom.

 Nature is me and all in one, and I am from a plant that the seed has harvested the earth to balance energy to grow.
The sun needs its own shield, as I orbit from land to space, I am shattered out of bound because I am without protection.

19

Don't touch my hair, as it means so much to me, oh Lord, tell them, please don't contact my crown.

As the music plays in my head, I am inclined to state, don't touch my soul as it is the rhythm of my own tunes to bear a beat to sing freedom.

It is not that we discover life; life has "discovered" us to space grace and become one with air. The oxygen of truth we breathe has a discovery and not a channel.
The wind tells a story as the breeze will blow out that it flows. I am of the skies with wings I fly.
Yesterday was a dashboard to display all my pain as I rewrite her in new details; she was purchased unedited and unaccompanied with a receipt to be refunded. The credit we give to self is not the same as our corrections, as the wind is no different from the sun that outsets the moonlight. I am as free as a bird to fly above the blow of the wing.

Detonations of a quote that reads, we are dying from the minute we exit the wombs of our founding mothers.

As a consolation to self, the branch is rotten once it shoots out fruits, and the labour of that birth is to be- rebranded from another.

So I was born to die as the world would call me a universal donor.
I am refusing to give unto you, my blood.
To repackage on your worth of life. To extend what was- written in stones from the wombs of the interior. Death is unavoidable.

Death stings yes, it runs tears and leaves the vessel empty and out of bound. As the body to a plane, it is like a flag flown at half-staff cold. The temperature still brings and bears the heat. Death is an under turn like true love; it hurts.

The exterior sits in on a bed to hear the man of fathers, the priest say, Lord, please bless her life and give safe passage unto the soul of being. Extreme unction is why I should beg for mercy on my soul.
After all, the drippings of my stained blood, I am gone as a gift I am truly sorry I didn't give it to you.

Why should I give me to you?

- Blood is the topic of discussion; my own drippings that drop from me.
- I should give me to you why?
  The drained liquid is it that I should disburse and still kill me? Further, as I am a banana in rot and an apple delicious to brown on the inside, I deteriorate.
- Shame to purpose, I am here yes to be of service, but service is for me to watch you pass your time on earth, not to change the process to one's death.

Vision 2020

You cannot put a timeline on blindness as you are an idea to see clearly- for greatness to come to past.

"The word is valiant, as it is noble. I am defined by you."

"Brave"

Life teaches you many things; no one is in your life permanent as they will temporarily move on from you. You must do the same. As you will learn to level down to match the person that is standing shorter than you, you will level up to match the length of the person standing taller.

Covered:

Grace is not from yesterday's pain; it is from today's desires to get to peace of mind.

As we uncover that a book contains a cover to open a page, we are one and the same to reflect on that same page.

Introduction:

Quote:

"I cannot stop my thoughts, but I can control my. Own actions in doing and creating the best version of beloved."

Preface:

The surface, the foreword, the preamble, the prologue, and prelude

Snippet:

A small detail to access me, yes, all in one, as you read me, I am open to the same air of the same oxygen you breathe.

Synopsis:

The brief tale to generalize all I can give to you of me.

So here, I am in a breakdown to access and give detail to my description. As I wonder, you will come to discover. The truth is one word in a million pieces and gives you billions of meanings to feel. If only escaping pain were that easy to a name, I wouldn't need to find me to a means.

"Edited"

Some things in life are just too long for a caption.

I spent a few days in the joint. I wasn't smoking shyt. I was-quarantined while I was -incarcerated for a crime to no action. So I know some things are genuinely too hard to caption.

I wouldn't change one thing about myself as many will place a caution sign to see themselves safe from my entrance to arise.

I hold pain to that same yellow, as betrayals have won on many days. The pain still tells the story of love on the inside of beloved.

The season was a pain to an outbreak, as I wear the same scars to cover.

We live in a world where the pain is not absolute or obsolete; it tells no tales other than broken. It will come from the day you started feeding it and ends when you stop.

Anecdotes the things we hold on the inside of us is black to beauty.

Rushed:

My mother's pain tells a story. The truth of her own pain reveals a tale.

- Pain shows her weakness, as she is the layers from the moon to cover the earth from burning.
- I cannot just journey and fly to space as my mind most days is on outer Mars. I need to find Neptune; maybe she will connect with me.

Welcome:

I have dared myself to wear gratitude like sin wears clothes. Like a cloak, I feed shelter as the rain poureth on me.
I am not wet, only damped from the breeze blowing.
Like most -opulent, we maintain access to our values as we never explain our cost.

As faith is the creator of things seen and heard of, I have learned to turn all my wounds into the idea that gives provident as it means wisdom is my birthday.

As I was stuck on triple sixes with no values to move, I found seven to break that very curse of wickedness to my soul. As the same access to triple twos and triple threes, fours and five reads an odd number to seven, the universe speaks again.

We will run to what cannot save us nor free us, as no one stays with you permanently, you will learn to survive on your own.
I have kept my own composure to the views of man as they were the betrayers of me and helped create my pain.

As I am a composer in writing out my own thoughts, I use things to know the sounds of a pronoun to get me to discourse myself. My name is Alecia.

As price is an option to tell a story, it reads the same pain and hurts no different from yesterday, to the unwanted madness of life.

I am here for your views and what experience has to offer.
As the entire is to a whole and complete, I am focused on the hopes of yesterday to not repeat on tomorrow's account.
Like paprika to the flavour, I am the colour to stain a pleasant good day to self and others to view.

Freedom won because, like love, it tells a story.
The change was never a question, but the pain was a way to suppress and not heal from what causes broken.
 Beloved, please free me.
Grace, please discover me.

Alecia Smith:

The age of man is no different from yesteryear.
As I have cometh to view and perceive this raw thing call madness, my mind is now elevated from 10% into a vast 8% as I am in a decreasing state of my own mind.

I was- asked, how can you say you are in a vast 10% and decreasing at the same time?
-      Well, when I am asleep, my thoughts are still going. When I am awake, I am trying to remember my -own dreams. As my -own mind as passed the night, it has gotten to today before me.
Hope wasn't looking to polish me clearly, as I am unpolished too my own- state of madness to change. I am unedited to pain, and I bear a particular shame to be un-ashamed by.

Mother:

Mother, they say purpose is oxygen, and I suddenly get high off my own supply, but I am a dealer for loving you.

Many days I ask myself how I can use the temperament of what happened to you to express me, and I can't find words.

I have tried not to express hate for your mother because if she didn't give you up. I wouldn't have a queen like you to call my mother.

Pain:

Please forgive me in the ways of how I express my rage for your mother. As I am your daughter, I do feel your pain.

---.---------------

What I will write is the truth, pain that tells hurt like no other. As why was a question I didn't ask for no answer, she left you to suffer so I will prey on her corpse-like an animal. I was thinking of when I murder her in my mind. Again I am in madness to stress. phuck you.

I am intoxicated as phuck. The rain is falling on me, like a flow to thunder. I folded up the strike of lightening to kill. High off madness, there is no coke in me.
So why am I planning a service to tell the world that knew you as a loving soul you were a monster to my mother?
I have planned. A ceremony with grace and gave her to Satan as she had given my mother to rivers of sperm. And her "underage" body was left to become a vessel and a carrier too soon.

As you sip on tea and fancy your way in other men's lives, did you think of your daughter?

You made black look like a disgrace not good enough because she wasn't as light as your other children. She is like me, a victim.
The only difference between her and me. Is that I am much more toxic, what a witch of a mother you are.

I am sleeping. I am sleeping as I will research you when you are dust because it pains me now to search for you. I wasn't wrong to plan your exit. I wasn't wrong to call the coroners in my head to pick up your body. The same way you left my mother when she was a baby, granny, I have three living children.
You have a total of 17 great-grandchildren. I hope they never meet you, So you won't ever get to stain them.

" Please let me be an umbrella to catch my own thoughts, so you won't ask me what I am thinking nor doing because you presumed to know me."

Grape is in-bedded in me like blood to bleed the essence of a stain as you are greeting my rise to apply peace of mind to my new state of madness to escape and be- deemed to find myself.

I am here walking alone again, like Mary, after the death of her son.

I am a woman, yes, to walk in the sand and running's of rivers flooding away in drown.

Let it go and stand clear of all the closing doors; oh bwoy, I sound like an automotive or is an automated system, yes me my own self.

As my mind is firing to my -own dialect, I find people still looking at me to "state gyal why you chat Suh bad."

Null and void, without legal force, as my madness is invalid, to my existence to be nonexistence to my pain amounting.

 As the pain is nothing but sadness and grief to upset me to know the unbalance, dysfunction to fault my- own self as nothing will give me power than the efforts of my own powerless thoughts.

As you're in the secular decrying state of your own mine to state, I am not qualified to write my madness in the fashion.

I chose it because I lack the meaning of education in inputting on what the rules are in writing.

Yes, I have broken your rules not to punctuate my -own thoughts because it doesn't have a break just a flow; in additional findings, just what is it that makes you different from me?

As you want me to be- educated by uneducated methods of my mind

She is more intelligent than me, my own self, so I will "not" dear myself, to have a conversation with "her."

Like the stars in the skies, freedom wasn't a pro-choice in my mind to stay in the elements of to run away from I cannot understand.

Please smell my bad breath and let me breathe that phucked up odour on you to see if you like the scent.

Now be a dear and tell me how did it feel to smell my pain and have it breathing on you?
You are no damn better than the enslavers of my capacity, so please sit and think while I express me like a coffee to drink, and allow you to ask me for a sweetener to trouble your blood count to sugar.

As you are troubled by my views of brilliants and being- broken with a mind of an abuse-

Please again let me state my mind and not my mindset, which is a set of things of my layers of insecurities to spot my reflection. To now ask of you to please touch on education again, as the thoughts proceed to process provident to knowledge, but not knowing reality is a relay in the dysfunctional madness to gain.

As a sister once tossed a set of shade on me as my character was now in question. As her post-state, there is nothing more than a confident woman who doesn't pretend to be something she is not. I was inclined to ask if madness is an act of depression because I would love it because I wouldn't be in pain anymore.

Da Reborn Mirror of Her
Her Raw Burden

"The execution of a burden is a sentence to murder one's pain. I am the chair to sit as I am being- electrified; to the electrocutions of my -own mind, I am reborn."

As the boat set sails on my -own thoughts as time is not- yet wasted or "waisted," I am fighting beloved to free all the spark plugs in one's mind to identify "grieve" and grief.

To: Tell it My mindset has no attritions to my state of mind, as I have held on to pain until today. So phuck you.

I have externalized to hurt me, my own- state is to state I was depressed by the madness of my shadow, but I cannot tell you why.

I am becoming "grace" to save Alecia.
So, like the boats sailing on the docks of my mind as I see the waters as a view of reflecting on the beauty of my own mind. Like water sailing as the fogs on the windows gazed at me into interpersonal.

As I see beloved to call my friend once-
As the ice-cold breeze hits the buildings that still stand in my mind.

As an enemy to blockers dimming the beauty. To see the recompense of payment to reward. The remuneration to the compensation of madness all in one meaning to the word pain.

The beauty of my mind is like birds flying and giving a feed to my thoughts of beloved, as I can tell hate you are not winning.

I am becoming like a boat in my mind sailing and leaving a trail, as I become imperfect to get to perfect, my beauty just informed me I am everything of gold.

Spread your wings. Nothing is genuinely impossible.
I am her as raw as a burden to be reborn, so please let me fly.
I am surrounded by doves. As I became free to fly beyond all things, I was -advised. By my wings, you may get shot down and be- subjected to bleed the essence of a drop of red as wine still stains on my teeth to rinse each drip of bitter grape.

As I have "learnt," there are many things to be accomplished in one night and learn about the next day. I am her raw again like a burden, as the money in my pocket means nothing but a sin to carry murder of my past enslaved by owners of my own thighs. Beloved free me and let me release all essence of water because I am beyond for you to respect and as organic as the integrity of a Goddess, my eyes will be lost to you in a dream never to wake up. I am -captured so again, free me.

Love is undeniably not supposed to hurt, but my God, love is everything of pain that breaks and stabs you on a daily and gashes on the inside of your own heart to bleed. Love is not as beautiful as they say it is energy filling and heart boiling; love is untreatable madness to cure and compel one's heart to compare a sense of feelings.

The eyes of the Lord are upon me as I am as unrighteous as the darns of the day trying to find one's "virtuous" state of mind, my heart is open to my cry as he will hear me when I do cry out to him.

I am colourful with pain as the circle of beloved is round. I am like a square in distress looking to become.

I have locked my hands with a friendship of my palms. To clasp my hands. in one and together to become as this will only be for today.

As our energy will cross and I will become handled by my madness. Like a door, open me up and let me be free as I will dive into swimming into drowning. I am lost at the nob to turn me around into what is called- the ashes to burn.
As the stars become a band with one heart burdened and beaten. By what is not known to her, her ownself as I rise with the thoughts nurture and the breeze is speaking out loud, I am feeling the breeze to blow, and I am not declining the miracle to love me my -own self in silence of what is and what is right as I cure beloved again.

I am you round and around professing my love unconditionally. I give myself unto you as I will subscribe. My loyalty unto you once not as an ultimatum, but I am trusting in me as a dedicated warrior I wasn't hunting to not prey but free me from the wild of unlove. As I found a lion to kiss my lips and smooth my heart, I will mellow my roar.

The lioness is undulled, and the refraction as me in a deflection.

As I am on a detour to run away from myself with pain. To grow, as yet to one's mind to process madness as it is still determined to be freed by and from my -own brain, oh, Lord, it is in need of corrective methods to give unto actions of one's pain again and free oneself again from hostage.

As my head is in an aching state of distress, I need a prescription.

To ensure my hurt as it was too much of A night of red stain and reminders to be examined, my vision to see that I was drunk by 9:30 P.M. and phucked up by 10:00 P.M.

My sin is institutional to drank more to know if I am ready.

To hunt again for Veronica

As Lisa has cometh to see the fogs in her eyes. As the dust of too much pain is gathered.

To, reflect darkness from the sand. In her eyes of pain.
I cannot flush it away to remove, but as I rub my fingers, I see the particles that drip the grains of what was keeping me unholy as the infection of touching the wounds of abrasion increases my eyes of pain.
I am blind to see my -own damage from Veronica.
Frigid and cold, I drowned in pain under the frozen "ice" of hail drops as it was as raw to the burden, and I still managed again to look into my own eyes as the tears cannot be -melted as it is too far gone, and it is still cold.

Lasered:
My eyes are surgery to pain open to burning as most days.
I am fragile but not delicate to pain as my face was once -covered with powder.

I am now free like a bird in the skies of beloved wearing me naked and open to see, as the glow of pain is no longer my friend, but the essence of wine is still my sin.

I drink her yet again like a red lipstick to stain me today. My sister, my twin, drank seven glasses of tainted as the pain served to blossom it was as if I graduated with a degree of shame and anxiety as the thoughts were telling me I will continue to suffer.

My journal   Alecia Smith

My name is Alecia Smith:

As it was a government name given to me by my mother and father, but I would rather it if you call me beloved. As a queen is befitting to my crown, I am- uplifted to prey and reign.

As there is a God on the inside of me, I need him to use me. But for me to allow him to use me, I must- really be used by him.
As I genuinely don't want him to use me for the glorious things. But like the drunk, I am to find care.

As my entire life was a lie said to me by my external being and nothing of my -own inside.
I have defeated so many demons and is still fighting Veronica in the darkest of times. I have cometh to know my worth, and I now understand what I deserve. I know what I am fighting for, and it is grace.

I will no longer entertain, or worry about man's opinion that has ridicule my own existence in a laugh. I am on God's timing to change.

As I have cometh to know love and genuinely love, whether it's different or "difficult" or unkind, I know the unconditional one I have is beloved as it is as incredible as the air we breathe from God.

Wearing Her Raw

DA REBORN MIRROR OF HER:

Her Raw Burden:

I used to have this luminous smile. I felt it was captivating to my glow, but the pain took it away and left me so empty.

I feel broken had me as I had many things to often cry about. But I cannot stop the thoughts of how much I love this picture.

The act of my own secrecy is now un- private to tell my truth.
-All Rights Reserved by Alecia Smith:

I cannot bounce my madness in the shadows of unknowingly knowing that God gave me a burden to be reserved.

As the thoughts of beloved, my own "VAGINA" needs to be investigated as a property that is conducting duties for my Estate of an un- proper to improper sale to carry a burden raw.

I am giving unto you the access to be permitted by my madness of permissions to enter me raw.
  As I am now in the principles of uncovering the raindrops from my mind into intellect.
  Please let me know if you're able to withstand the rain?
As madness has now been- classed as a licensed sickness, I am as raw as the light of day.

As my own admission will give you access to my pain and sorrows, I must say I am the truth, and I am here to now inconvenience your new "correspondents" to your emotions.

So please don't look at yourself as the reflections will help you become your true self. As you know, we are beloved, but in the entry to be carried to the façade of not real. I must say I do not wish to provoke you as you hate your own existence.

As the madness you will inherit is not to be embezzled, please proceed into me again raw, like a **vacuum** without bags attached.

I am -her raw.

_Dearly beloved, as we are gathered in the precautions of my mind to read my burden, please let me unveil myself to you as the cautionary to my thoughts is indifferent to average your account.

My mind is thy journey as my pain has now teleported my consciousness beyond the doors of this point.

42

Please take your time because she is un- fragile to shame and sins her madness.

She will soon let you in undoubtedly as her burden is a volume.
Due to the behavioural patterns of lack of sleep, I was- told melatonin is the new "Ambien" to rest.

I am not an addict, addicted to the substance of I must subscribe to sin and drown in knowledge, as the mind tells me. So, let's continue the conversation, and please do share all the feedbacks of our madness.

As the continuation of her journal continues to the free borne illness of her own- site again to herself-
I am at lost to tell myself never to talk to strangers. They will clutter your mind, with the façade of care, and make your own thighs become a charity not to know clarity.

I have told sin to phuck itself and give me a digital discount to being faster to my own death in contemplations to archive Veronica.

My twin sister, the drunk as she held the keys to access my data and become the asset to my pension to collect me and still place me in sin again.

I was now -archived by her as she is as wicked as the daylight to the sun. Again, I am in sin as the vacuum of human tongues is still a destroyer to a cleanse of my own body's worth.
Saliva is the ship to my own body. God, please save me.

I was born perfect, but as I grew, I took on all imprisonments of my imperfections. Yes, the hands of my enemies that were placed upon my life to say I shall disappear and dishonoured God because he couldn't love me to let me suffer and feel pain. So now, let us forget about him and that he exists through me and for me.

The terms of things are my- own distractions, as my heart of selfishness and broken is here.

Instead of rendering God as my aid to become anointed in purpose, I am crying as if I don't want to be reborn.

Her Raw Burden:

Love is an incredible thing. But that same love is foolish as I notice that love is not only necessary to be glorified but to be beaten and broken by that conditional method. I am challenging you to be -used while you are rising to find beloved.

I have confined my lips with the devil of cherished as I viewed a kiss of silence to lie.

She was frightened to express to him she is in love but was acting out the rights of her true self as everything in her was inclined to cheat on her -own madness.

As she was discerning into an escape, as there is death on the tips of her own lips to tongue her own words of murdered by a kiss to a death sentence of uncurable but treatable by default.

Here comes the conversation again with the thoughts of beloved cheating in. And with the flesh of lips locked together as the covetousness of her- mind was the essence of unashamed. By rage and the fatality of a thing called kiss me again and kill me yet again. I will be rebirthed from ashes and feelings of lust to lock deceit of the lips of murdered by her beloved raw.

I am still sitting on Thursday thinking about Saturday as the date to my life will determine me and my- own state of unsound. As I break my fast and forget about Friday, here I am drinking poison to seal my -own lips with red wine.
The idiocy of "prized" is not a lie; it is a story of her listing all of her outer pain and betrayals.

Lord, as the soundtracks of pain, plays through the weekend in my own president. I am still crying to find freedom and discover grace.
 As "the days" of Thursday's had me on Wednesday's, yelling into Friday's and skipped days of the pain of there is nothing else in me.

45

As the air is no longer in need of me to breathe because I am out dry and withered away from unfreed.

 As my heart is still broken by madness, as I need to trust and believe the day will come when he will need me as I rise to let go of it wasn't meant to be. So I am over being lost.

God, was I giving all of me to madness for no reason? As he will never love me in ways of beloved. Freed by scents of stank, by the rot of burdened by the contamination of insertion; wounded by default.

As the thoughts of me, my own self is having a conversation with, and my own self is beyond establishment.

As the invention of time is still in one and within. My own thoughts of like, I am like a weapon to shoot. I have cometh to know him un me.

As the human in me is like the rest of us- Prone to judge as the air of oxygen has never evaluated us, why do we "judge" and view sin like clothes?

To lie about one's past is to deny one's future in my then government of unstated, as my body is a story to age, but my face will never change because it wears pain like sin.
I have subscribed to the revelation of my own body and not the genesis of pain because it reveals many tales of un- coming.
 I am glowing below in a picture that shows. A lie of my outside as I was in pain of each day.

 The camera flash that told something else was a theoretical reflection of my- own tooth on a glass of whatever. Just smile and look unbroken. If I were to confess -my iniquities.
 I will be judged by many if I confess my sins again that the almighty God is authentic, and he needs just to forgive me for all my sins should he cleanse me from unrighteous and not let the negative thoughts destroy me?

46

I need to maintain a positive attitude toward the external façade I created and just live.
There will always be a thousand-words to the reasons why I shouldn't sin.

As there are many justifications to my then state of crying, the thoughts of I should hold my head up high and keep on going when you have no clue of what I am feeling, is a question I shouldn't ask because you cannot answer me my -own self, yes.

It is almost like the outer of myself is always saying repay it with anger and never promise yourself any form of happiness, never make better decisions to live life because it is just a lie. You were- made to remain in your -own sadness.

I have freed hate, and now I have cometh to free love if love would only let me be released by it. As I am amazed by God's blessings, I am also being glorified by not to fear change.

_____I am Alecia Smith:

- _On the lips of a poet's lies the art to write one's heart on paper. As that paper will soon deteriorate to rot as the water will hit waves of damp in the rain.

-

Raw like a burden and wearing her like pain.
I am the madness to be victimized by pain; I am not sure why I am burdened by the looks of broken, as the greatness in me as a woman is required to maintain the integrity of madness as an ability to be mad.

As I know, not my worth, as the world treats me not as an option, but as an opinion to thoughts.
As nothing sees me in the light of I am in demand of love, as I cannot find beloved.

If I allow my madness to treat me like an option to measure choice, it will soon give me an equation to narrow my baggage to my -own luggage.

As I lack in the days of sleep to not know the pillows, I am as tired as the day to break as the sun lifts from the skies of pain.

God, please, before I call myself righteous and spiritual, let me find the kindness of my -own mind. Like starch, let me become sugar to stay and become sort.

As I tell kindness of my -own evolution to see beyond all things as pain is a feeling to feel as I can evolve with my- own thoughts.

As -I ask death not to leave me in the silence of a mystery. To die because when you fear what you cannot change, you fear the changes that are current fire is flames and blame as our souls cross and spirits have always travelled to its -own formation, I am in love with you God as I am finding becoming her.

Education is a souvenir, and not a burden as learning is a lesson even when pain is an enemy, it is still your teacher.

48

As knowledge is like tears in the rain and the seeing of things is a pain I cannot help myself but (2) glitter in the dark because all moments will soon be lost in time without finding beauty, as I am all cut up on the outside of me my -own self.

Evolution

I am provident as I must ask myself the meaning of such a word as I retained knowest of knowledge when my body speaks to me.
 It is foreign, yes, as I cannot end my -own thoughts because the consciousness of day is awakening before I break day.

Sprouted, I am ready to be made whole as a flower to the scent of an arrangement to bloom.

 I will blossom, but still, yet, I rot from my- own roots as the water scent is still musty and ole.
 I am not cleansed by or of dirt; I am even again in rot from my waist down.

"You cannot crown a king without crowning a queen."
The days of man have shifted to where men think of women as
possessions and not the carrier of I will bring forth the fruits of our
labour together. I am royal and becoming crowned to rule.
I am her leader and mother of many; I am her the volume to sound. Can
you hear me?

- The wings of the phoenix, who am I? I am her.
God, who -really controls the phoenix as I am in the world of unfree, but still yet I fly.

I am a bird that operates with a piece of what is my -own mind looking for a nest to call home each day as I burn each night.
I will arrive in a different dimension to tell a story of my red-lit on fire; I am the flames.

The serenity of my- own mind is a troubling sense to the rest of the world as my fire is always a smoke to put out a -conflagration. I am that smoke when you open up your door.
Since this is my seventh night to die, I must repent bringing my ashes peace of mind again.

Ashes have a scent when it burns, and still, yet, you will rise from it like fertilizer, it becomes a cure to heal. I am like that dust to wonder if I have a smell after each burning scent. As I become that new manure as they spread my body as it is, I become dirt of my- own ashes again.
My thoughts as a phoenix are now the new nitrogen to structure and improve on a new level of growth so as I fly ashes again to ashes I go.

Ashes to ashes and flames to flames I am burning. Still, I am forever the crow.
Like the phoenix, I rise to wander like the dust of my -own ashes; my name is her.

The cowardness in me has been awakened to love me, my -own self, with no intentions of ever loving her, me, my -own self.
As the bird with wings looks at me, she looks nothing like me but still, yet she is a woman younger but in pain.

As the scent of her body odour descended onto the surface of nothing short of what my burning smoke is doing to the air, I worry not about affecting flames as I rise again to live "life." I am forever the phoenix.

As I gave him everything in me and left myself empty, I will never give myself unto another since you took all of me without question.

As I opened up my -own mind to thought, I realize I was lusting after what was never going to notice me.
Each day I walk past me to reflect and look at her. As his wool was a shelter for her, and his seat was a safe place to her warmth.
He looks at me as I burn again, lit to flames as he lies still to the rest of my outer look.
Even today, with all of the lies, he is still foreseeing me to express real. But with a heart of unfairness, I buried him again in hate of what I cannot change.

I knew the cancer in him has no cure to heal because he is far from medicine. The essence of that promise was to compel me to die again as my wings grew tired of flying.

I knew I wouldn't rise on the eight sentences of my death since.
I cheated on him, the fifth of no conscience, and my subconscious -was at ashes length faded in the dust.

The thoughts of me flying away from life and formation of my dust will rebirth is a rise because I am no longer in the same place to be looked at as my -own scorn was my tormentation of my wings to fly.

53

Gosh, I am black with fire and bold with beauty, but my colour is still yellow to reflect dirt and maze of glaze that drips like starch tainted to a scent of sin.

–

DA REBORN MIRROR OF HER:
Her Raw Burden Vol#2.

I am colourful. I am more than black and white. I am my -own colours of the rainbow.

—

The pain is unreal as I cry in the middle of the gaze to wander. I am happy the fade tells a lie to my glow radiant to the beauty they call it. If only the image could see my inside open and understand what it means to see beautiful.

This look has me paying for something that I cannot cash out in coins but a firm peace of mind to glaze at sparks of lights.

The radiance of Alecia ignites a burning fire within my -own blazing fire that will never be -extinguished. I am a secret to tell a story about my -own self.

Affirmation Is unspoken to spoken.

The pronouncement is the vibrations of life and a breath of air that grace was- given to us from the Most -High, the "Omnific." As all words that cometh from him (is) clothes to my body and beauty of light to glaze my spirit to only, as I dear not to judge myself no longer because by judging my -own self. I am indeed sinning once more.

As my -own path of evolution is to guide my spirit to find my own shadow, and the environment is the earth of my own body to free me like grass growing. I am whole and at one with peace of mind.

As the springs of waters run through my -own body supply, I am like the infinite of grace and my heart is fully supplied with gratitude of the inner vibrations once more to live life.

- Alecia Smith

-

"When many individuals put you down, there is the inner version of yourself that's willing and ready to pick you up and uplift your inner thoughts to believe and stand even taller."

The truth is that whatever is -broken can be mended like a bad habit; you will lose it eventually. So give yourself time to let the healing process begin and rise out of that darkness stronger.

"The only way to ever produce greatness is never to settle; many speak of great work only bring about results. So love what you do to realize beyond your sight of a vision there is darkness before the light."

As you're thinking through life, there is nothing in the world more troubling than you being alone with your -own thoughts.

The poison that will kill the toxins of life is never to judge nor not to let anyone court you. Nor don't make your -own jealousy compete with anyone else.

All that is- required of you is just to focus on the best version of yourself.

Asking the inner version of myself to pour a fresh on me is like asking God on the inside of myself to become my actual self.
I am away from Alecia most days, and still, I am not sure how I fit.
Alecia is looking into the beloved thoughts of her own eyes to say to herself if you haven't cried, your eyes aren't beautiful enough.

So I have cried over and over again from pain nothing is real to me. The thoughts of broken lives within me like my mother, I was taken at hostage point forced into pain and was enslaved by methods of rage.
I was spiritually connected to grace enough to feel the connections of the trees and bound my body to the earth.
The unedited truth about myself is a journal within my -own head.

If you have ever read "her," then you will know of all my struggles and what hurts me.

-At the beginning of life, to the end of a walk, pain is not just a feeling anymore; it's a habit to kick like a harmful drug overdose.

That's how I live through my depressed state of what I cannot change and free myself from, but grace is- hoped to find who I am again.

Alecia is a real person. Veronica was a façade created from the middle of me, and she broke me on a daily. I am so unfree that I cannot breathe.

When I wrote "Her," I felt freed by a change to uncorrupt my pain and finally shame the uneven madness of what is a lie by all means. But as the dawn of light went out, I poured me another drink and found her a route to escape again. The thoughts of beloved is not a friend, is a problem to my -own soul as she is -lost at sea.

As a girl to not know my -own worth of innocence, I fear what the pain took away my -own state of stability to stay stable to my -own truth as I can bring nothing that he took away from me back to life.

I feared defeat had won at guiding me into a hostage point, and I cannot break away from her, because we are linked together, Veronica and Alecia. We are sisters and "as" one is sober, and one is a drunk to pain. The burden at this point is beyond raw to her because there is no going back ever again.

As each soldier in training enters a battleground, they learn all the essential rules toward discipline.

As a captain would say, if you start practicing making your bed at the first site of when you rise, you will begin to make progress toward your future and bring about change. Today is Saturday the day of the seventh day of rest as I rise in the elements of the Shabbat and give shalom unto my soul. I am still alive.

As grace is within me am not sure if I -am found other than I am living for today to gain.

As the day is shorter in the length of what I cannot change, I- am awoken from my -own foolishness.

I am a picture of black and white; I reflect a story to tell; I am- bitten with colour; still, my injustice is raw as the external beauty of glow was a look to maintain.

I was nowhere near my internal thoughts of I am never-ending to growing as I was only asking the wrong person to notice me and not seeing myself.

The mental notes to oneself are becoming, it is right I am unbalanced is the terms and conditions of a beautiful print read to me yes, for my -own thoughts to reflect on me as the image was -used up to fill a vast or vase they call it as the flowers of grass still rots.

I was calling God to ask if the condition was still rotten to the sights of me daily like a bad apple.

We are so much alike, you and me the signs of cancer we share like a research lab, we share results of madness that has apprehended my mind.

As our thoughts finesse the deceits of I must love as the essence of still finessing me is so undeniable.

Like I now know, pain is wearing me rotten and bold as you continue to hurt me beyond this point as others think of my thoughts as a plug. As to whether it's a dub to not happening is still being finesse.

I am like a forest running through my -own head. I genuinely view the leaves like a conversation in my brain space to have with myself.

Like each walk to a step. I am writing to me yes my- own self in an interview with my mind in my head as we continue to talk to each other here I was writing her.

As that conversation continues the thoughts of the breeze blew on me as the wind blows louder my discussion on paper continues with no break as my feelings did not end I am open like a bottle with a cork or an upgraded lid to look at in human eyes.

DA REBORN MIRROR OF HER:

Her Raw Burden Vol#2.

Telling- it all, nothing should be left unfiltered.
How you tell your truth is on you.

If you have read HER, in the languages of Arts, or the Queens English, then I guess you will then state. That I have broken the rules in the ways of American writing, by not adequately, nor appropriately punctuate any forms of my sequences to a sentence.
Please let me convey my thoughts to you in the madness that you cannot structure pain, because it is a conversation to surface sounds and flows to unbalanced.

In the madness- of becoming

 As you think of the exterior, your interior constructs things differently. Yes, as the external is unbrave and is somewhat unbold to the truth, I wrote again in a conversation as it was befitting not to tell a story, but express my pain to oneself.

- - Don't add to anyone else's timeline in the ways of how you choose to compose your thoughts.
- Being in control of you is sacred and is of high value.
- The stories we have within us sometimes are painful and hurts, but the truth is we are that story to tell.

- Many persons state, they don't have a religion, nor do they believe in God. As I can only remember God and care nothing about the thing that divides us as a people, I wonder if God wants me to practice going to church because I hate going. My body is searching for the grace of what I cannot belong to nor want.
  -

The truth is my therapy to myself as I write all of me on a piece of paper.
The uncensored truth is I am always afraid of when I am through with writing all that comes to me because I don't know what I have unleashed on paper if it is -really the real me.
- Most days, I want to ask my -own self for a divorce, because I cannot understand her. Nor do I want to.
- The utmost important "thing" in my life is my kids, and I cannot understand why I am disappointed or feel like I am disappointing them.
  -

I feel like I don't have enough time to cherish with them because I have killed myself with madness. So today, I decided to book an appointment with a therapist to express myself.
As I cannot and will not lose myself to the façade of madness again.

I don't want to tell this therapist I hide and drink myself away because I am afraid of my self.

As I am a person in makeup and once I unravel myself I cannot recognize the real person within myself, I depend on Veronica to aid me, but today I had to tell myself all I need is me to be ok.

As a person asked of me to meet the real me and unveil my beauty

I wanted to ask of them if they are at beloved because nothing about my outer layer is beautiful. Just as how he hasn't seen God. But he loves the very beauty of God's presence; that's what I am on the inside, beyond my wrap.

-   Different:
-   Everyone has a book in them, how you tell the story is essential.
-   It states in time once you ring the bell, you cannot "un" ring the bell, so yes, I am really different.
-   I am different from this standpoint, and I am here to state that I have a problem.
-

My name is Alecia. I am an addict. Stating that I am an addict with a problem is one of the toughest decisions I have ever come in contact with.

I am different, yes, as I worry, so do I journal hope to gain her freedom, as it was only yesterday, she cried for inner love. She is still not yet freed, as a wall is always a walk to find a door to open, I am her.

Different yes, like water, most days I which(wish) I was blue, but the subtlety of my life is different. Yes, as it still means my qualities are in an argument of distinction, so I am away to embrace again diverse.

The lessons to life are always stated with compassion to do the right thing; how it doesn't matter in the end is a mystery because, like the pain, we fear the things that hurt us in the end. The thoughts of I once existed before today is a pain as I cannot remember the garden of my mother nor the flowers of what they call a sunflower.

 What I do have is a stain to rinse and clothes me forever in pain. As the will dawn before, it lights out so will my heart, and it will become bleak out like a night due to dew from the raindrops of water falling through the night of yesterday's love of God. If only I could wake and stay in the set of that era.

My conscience is in a troubling state of mind with the guilt I feel as I tried to correct an error that wasn't my mistake; the mirror to rule is not wrong, but the pain is right.

-The truth has no bearings to tell a lie only to escape winter as it will soon snow again in fall as October is way too cold as I love him. Once more again, not only in a dream but in reality. As I will glaze into a blaze of what is not eyes but holy spirits, God has just touched me again in arms of length, and I am awake still yes.

- Heritage of all things that betrays me in death. I must come back to life after death; I rise again.

-Erase all essences of a "scent," it is not a perfume but a mould of sin-stained discharge from a night of revenge on my VAGINA. I am not my scent, but his smell is now my perfume as he was the one that left me with an essence, and a stain tainted in another sin to behold and not love rage I recreated and the story he told in-between my thighs.

- Racing to find God as he is in me, my saviour.

The mirror is not only a reflection of its genesis.

Smaller than life, she is still that same little girl:

The little girl in the mirror that frequently.

Sits in the dark of her madness between. Her and rational thoughts of. The disorder of insanity. Which is her sickness?

The disconnections of the mirror keep her in a bipolar state of mind with dark liquor, the alcohol of not pure water, but everything of a toxin with pure poison.

As you have read her. The addictions of my mind "want" many things, the thighs of -my soul "wonders" with pain. As I "lust" my way at a list of men that I wonder if any is different from my abuser. The mirror is not just a glass; its what keeps my reflection in a daze to reflect pain again.

- She had a meeting with God to express her thoughts of her madness as she writes all of her, which one of herself is she today is still a mystery as she loves many men through a call or a text states I love you with my outside.

- Today Lisa is still in space, wondering if she is "in" Mars as her phone proudly rang to update her of her appointment with the doctor. As she proudly confirmed the date as another, she is still not herself the girl in the mirror.

- Welcome:

In the essence of welcome is my praise to rise and welcome God as the head of my life.

My name is WHY warrior next to God and queen warrior of a village I am here to lead the victory of grace to elevate and become my true self.

The tribe of my mother, I don't know. As her lineage was -never explained to her as I am searching. So I shall teach her and my children. Who we are as queen nesters of warrior's and hunters to lead as my ancestors before me had a lot in them to give, and I need to develop it all into my soul as well as to honour them.

As well as show gratitude to them because I cannot repay the sacrifice, but I can pay it forward.

For I am no longer a slave, was an expression for yesterday as today in the twenty-first century; I am an upgraded version of free to pass by. I am an updated version from the beginning. So I shall be in the end as it 'sits now in Genesis.

I am living in all things of destruction that should overcome its day in revelation.

 I am in the eras of the error to correct because the fallen angels and blockers of prayers are on the rise.

Yesterday I was praying harder than I did before because I was afraid of the not coming to past, but God was readi-

I am -healed by grace; victory is good to me. God is my motivator praise be to me voice of a screaming call open up my mouth and speak to him in honour of I will worship you cry.

If I had become you, I wouldn't have met my true self; I am not you.
I cannot be you; I can only be me the lioness of the hunt and the waters of the sea I am reborn.

To the crown of body sin, I am now alkaline because my body's PH no longer contains you, I have come to rinse you once more.

As I am in the essence of rain and lightning bolt thunder what will strike when God is readi, I don't know as I pray for safekeeping's, I still need a shower to rinse me holy to grace and uplift peace.

-   Education:

Most days, I am at a standstill because I cannot express myself in ways and meanings I don't think I am where I want to be. The thoughts of confusion are my friend on a daily to aid her is a huge problem.

In life, as an educational factor on me, not achieving a degree unless it is measured as a measurement is thought to self, so most days, I am afraid to open up my space of mind.

So my methods of doing this are different, so here I am now 37 years of age wanting to go back to school because I want to be able to achieve success. As I look at others, I am still at a wonder as Christ had a different knowledge I am not sure of what wisdom I have.

So like the great, Mandela stated, the power of knowledge is a win, which is my intake. As my voice is still silent to a read, but now I will write myself as unashamed of not having a degree because it doesn't change me, I am still me filled with ideas and grace.

<u>Each drop</u> is every "droppings" of pain I am still a victim yes as heaven is still in my mind to reach-
Like the circle of one glass, I am still drowning beyond flow.

I found myself telling another of the feelings between the sound of his voice-
As I dream of him most days- I created the façade of madness. It was my shame, and not his because he doesn't know me at all; he only knows the idea of me. As he expresses all that was in me, and nothing was for me.

Freedom won

- <u>Acknowledgment:</u>

The principle of life is to tell yourself you are better than the day before as I acknowledge my purpose; I am not here to settle.

I would like to thank you for creating me in your light and truth to grow from a seed into a root to sprout fruit.

To the man that took me in and help me become a woman in my own right-

As I wasn't ready for life, to LIVE in you created a path for me to let go of my pain as we grew on the strength of I believe in myself and not what others think of me to excel beyond all I can do is "live."

To my mother, my queen, I cannot express how much I love and appreciate you for being my rock to stand on and teaching me the importance of paying it forward in life.

To my father, I love you for being there in my life to see me become a woman now and learning the critical core values of what family is and continue to enjoy them no matter what.

Freedom won

Why?

I am in love with someone that will never love me?
So here I am listening to sounds of to love someone that will love me,
but I found nothing but a wall placed at the tunnel to fight.

My heart to broken, as I cannot "express" my why's I fear darkness will
take me over before love ever captures my soul because my body is
vastly inadequate to live life and has no comfort to find peace.

As anything of music. Will play a sound in the tongues of my sea of a
cat to drown me.

As a puss on two legs has destroyed my world to breathe, why?
Here I am in the elements of what they call a soul tie of what is termed
sex with the enemy.

A soul tie is an essence to the foundations of another. And I am that
element to myself to take in all of me—the celibacy of my body
exchanges through my mind.

Oh lord, I never knew I was -corrupted by the essence of my rapist and
my molester.

As I took their scent of stains in my spirit. All of what destroyed me,
the river of the garden of what was able.

Please Forgive Me:

If I am not like you.
Why do I believe in the elements of not writing in chapters, because
internally, your mind is moving it's not breaking to section all that is in
you it's thinking ahead of life?

I honestly cannot chapter what takes all of me to tell it all in pain.

My thoughts flow like a beat to the rhythm; it doesn't have a break like
a body, its God, and you in one having a moment to capture not fancy
up to lose but to recreate a vision to rise on the sound of noise.

Freedom won

Like pain, it is the energy used up to feel, so if you continue to feed it, it will never stop, it will continue to another level of hurt and frustration.

The elements of my mind rise before me with God, my creator, so I want to be awake to catch all that it's offering in service of prayers.

Knowing:

You become what you attract, what you are surrounded by defines you and your methods of life.

The thoughts of energy are contagious choosing who you will give yours to is essential.

The choosing of your self is to become the elements within the environment of your own body, so be careful of what seed you will plant in you, it may never grow is thought to a sound, so why do things like everyone else.

Freedom won

The prayer:

The thoughts of my prayers to you lord as my spirits discerns into discernment of the same elements of my judgment, and I am alive.

As the refinement of grace giveth to me each day a new day~

The sophistication of my thoughts is alive, and well as each moment I laid, I am upraised by a rebirth to be reborn.
The subtlety of my journey into enlightenment is wisdom to speak all over my blessings.

"To whom much is given to be of service. so much more is required to be done and shall be done in fate and by fate."

We rise to fall, fall to "Rise" like no other, as sin is for us all let us all pray in an assemble to correct life again and give God praise.
As all great warriors of life had something to say about "life."
God inspired and (Aspire) all great men to walk the earth.
A quote from the great is that in the end. We will remember not the words- of our "enemies" but the silence of our friends.
Everything we have come to trust in is the system that breaks us as citizens of God.

As darkness cannot drive darkness only the light of God and all forces from him, as the same methods of talks that hate cannot drive hate.
The elements of love will change all things.
The teachings of (He) "is" love and love is him.

I am having a beautifully "mentioned" conversation with and of my inner thoughts of the omnificent creator of all powers and life force connecting me throughout the universe.

I am the beginning to no end is your reign, what you have touched, and crowned upon my head as a throne to a cover I dear not to remove until I have mastered and preserved the body of my temple.

Freedom won

As the enemies of my life have set thorns upon my scalp, you have revealed my path to unlock it all to know more in the bondage of my thoughts freedom is alive and well, and I am free to praise glory be to God.

I am in the elements of peace and safekeeping.
My Peace of mind and command to stand, walk but not run is a travel, and a way to not get lost are now my elements to make it home.

God, I know all you have ever wanted from me is to see my worth because you know my values, in searching to find patience and inner peace to heal oneself.

I am no longer in search of my worth because today I pressed play, and my values were on display.
So, my saviour, here is my prayer to you!

Dear God, I am so grateful that you have inspired me. To dream on the inside of me and to understand that you live on the inside of me.

As, well as on the outer layer of pain. And the inner heart of my healing place calls the home of peace in the sacred gardening of safe.

Each day of my life.
I take on with the most utmost respect for the gratitude of life.
To live in your presence as a reborn warrior to a different level of myself.

The inner truth of life has been my true blessings to wake up and see I have you carrying me to the finish line as a child to you I am- humbled by the benefits I am receiving from you.

You have been my covenant where the heavens of my "Temple" is at peace each day I see myself as my spirit takes me to new levels in life.

Each morning I am uplifted by grace to run to a starting line because you are carrying me to a surface of what is my preface into life.

Freedom won

As I introduced to holy and beauty, Lord, as I surrender my soul to you in shouting, I am renewed by your blessings each moment in time and with time to each your amazing grace.

I welcome hope and kindness in the path of my life because I cannot and will not only live for myself but live in dreams of tomorrow to give you all of me in grace and to know I am no longer -burdened by the thing they call my shame.

Yesterday was the most substantial of your raindrops.

As the showering falling as lives were- taken into the soils of. The earth there was also the remaking of another.

Oh lord, I am not a sinner was my question, as I stand in silence and pray for "grace" to hit my head.

As the water hit my forehead again it washed away my mask, and I had used to cover up each spot on my face as I watched the foundation of dirt drilled from my face, I looked up at grace to hold me in one place.

As I was still standing and not moving, I was in the land of water; praises had me at worship and, I wasn't at war or thinking of my murder.

As I got wet, the flood of change embarked upon me to change me oh God and make me more like you, your amazing hands touched my face and stated I am who I am a child as you're not ready to carry what I have for you your training must continue.

Freedom won

Dedication:

This book is devoted to my first "Love" and my king Rayden and my beautiful queens Nevaeh and Amanda.

I cannot express all I have to be thankful for in loving you, the system of support I have in you I cherish within eternity, and the ending of my reign where you will lead as leaders as my spirit carries -over you. I dedicate all of me to you as you are my Nubian beauties.

As you have come to remake me your mother, I cherish the title to be called. And I will always be a mother and your mother to bear. I am getting ole, and as my ole soul will be descending into particles I give unto you three pieces of me, and your sister to honour us by as I will not be gone but around know that I have retired my earthly self to be at peace with the spirits of my pure shadow.

As I "right" all that is in my heart, I am super proud of my queen Nevaeh for growing up and understanding life and the worth of values in reverse to be kind and thoughtful enough to pay it forward as a leader.

My crowned charm Amanda I live to rise for you to hear your voice blaze into the darn of each "mawning" as you "sung" with grace to render soul of which is ole. I am within the reflections of myself through you, and I am living again to rise.

Rayden as a "KING" let no man tell you of what your worth is, you are a God and a leader, a lion, to hunt and protect.

As a black man know you will be tested and put to the test, but I am equipping you with a legacy of grace to be ready, as our ancestors fought for freedom, you will have to do the same for your sons and daughters.

Freedom won

Knowing we are not free only have passes to travel still in this error I
cry for you daily as I cover you with my blood and the Goddess cry,
you will be a reigning leader as I was and will always be your mother.
To my queen, at first, I didn't understand why and how you could find
the courage to rise, then I became a mother, and I see your sacrifices to
make it through the stormy weather.

Knowing a woman carried you and left you, my mother, I pay respect,
because she made it possible for me to be and become your daughter.

So, I thank her for you-you had me at age 22 you were giving birth to
me, we are so much alike and destined by fate, you wouldn't understand
if I tell you, mother, I am your do-over.
As you are "mines," I am yours, my queen.
The love I have for you is in between God and beloved.
I salute your mother for having you because you are nothing short of a
miracle from God; you're a seed planted in purpose.

To my king, I will walk with you as long as you hold my hands until
the end of time, where our spirits will re-merge, and our bodies
reconnected where our souls will find peace. I love you beyond today,
and yesterday, you are my reason.

Freedom won

Intake call
Synopsis:
Here I am reborn.
"What does it mean to say I am reborn"?

=====================================

Everything of freedom and love. No fear, the inner strength to begin at the start of opening up my -own door into the success of the mind and body.

Where does my soul go once? I embrace life is within me a future. Yesterday I was having a "conversation" with my soul.

As my heart informed me to stop awaiting others to celebrate me, as I need to set all my goals in place to achieve my self-worth and gain, and I should always clap myself in the end to a victory.
As I am telling myself this, I am not in the clear until I am free as bondage has us, and I am a part of the unfear. I found a quote to define as a person.
God is the reason why I feel the pain to smile even when I am confused by the process to rise and look ahead of change.

The truth is that life is not just about finding yourself; it is about discovering God and the reason why he created you.

As I express to myself, we will be doing a lot of walking away-because it will do us justice.

Reborn is just not about waking up and living in the day, and it's about being grateful that you have paved the way for self to rise again, and dream as all is not lost.
As we often don't break our silence about pain, it carries us into the wild of unsound.
We are and were two people in love; then. Pain happens, the one not to express nor explain. I am not upset at myself because I cannot change what I have done nor what has happened to me.

Freedom won

What am I walking away from?
I am walking away from my rage to get angry-
Happiness is "a" look to maintain internally and mentally, and it becomes hope to elevate change and purpose.

I am not looking for a look to glow, but I am looking for the risk to take a chance to no longer be unbothered by unhappiness- because I don't need unsafe but a safe temple to call home.
As I question the methods of change, I am not afraid to accept him, who is the head of my life, God.

Preface:
Preface means foreword as it's the same as an introduction, yes.
I am a woman, yes, that is beyond measure. The pain is nothing and everything, yes, and here is my preface to her pinned in pain as I am now reborn.

I was- told to use myself as a class, so I asked myself, what have I mastered other than pain?
I was now- informed yes, that's a degree to recognize madness of. Pain, so I look up, and there was a mirror reflecting my state.

Why reborn as a method to settle and title myself was to gain me in becoming my strength. I was no -longer mutated about my pain.

I knew the transformation was everything I needed to become in the end.
I needed to become wiser as a person, a queen and a leader.

Every night I am in pain because I see him.
I cannot remember his name. I know where he lives, and then I know nothing of him now as he placed me on my knees to rape my mouth; what do I know of foreplay at 16 as my body is so young. I don't even know it.
As he watched me for hours on my knees, refusing, he left me there to think of my escape.

Freedom won

I rise not to want Alecia to open up like any other but only myself.
I rise above the methods of peace to know and honour my duties as a
queen of the universe.

I am the master to co-create myself with God as the head of me and my
voice to survive.
I am a victim, yes, I know, but today I am tired as I have warned too
many in my head to murder. I must let go.

Freedom won

A Table of Context I don't have to label what shouldn't be sectioned by rules, but here is my listing to express my why's.

My methods:
- -
  - -Psalms: the book that holds all my notes to the truth.
  -
  - -Genesis: The beginning   "PAIN"-
  -
  - -Beloved: In love with all aspects of my internal grace.
  -
  - Me: Treasured.
  -
  - Inner truth: Central all I "have" with all I can.
  -
  - Escape: Running away from my madness.
  -
  - Revelation: Where do I go next.
  -
  - Freedom: I am no longer at a hostage point in my life.
  -
  - Grace: In service to pray between God and me.
  - Rise: To raise the death of pain and a façade created by man to view me in.
  - Angered: By many methods of shame.
  - Buried alive in many secrets of shame to find beloved in a dream again to shame.

Freedom won

The scars of pain is still a gash that has left me with a scrape of a pointing edge of bruises and even all cut up. As you cry, please note freedom is not coming, as my blood dripping is in a bleed of freedom to surface.

-I am sorry for your loss, or is it lost?
The TALK to a conversation stating that words are universal is a beauty just like music; it brings us all together.

- -The trail to the madness in my head is worded just to save me from myself, and I know it's a walk, but at least I am not thinking about suicide as I repeat the same methods in my head each day saying I am sorry for my "own" loss.

- - I have lied to myself and my FAMILY. They don't -really know me.
- - As in the same, I don't remember my self.
- I am sleeping in a lot lately as I am afraid to face the truth about my self.
- As I am listening to the sounds of music again in my head as I am not worried about one thing other than my selfish methods of I don't want to do better.
- I am sitting in the madness of what I cannot change to make sense of as a recap in my head daily, I am so out of place with

Freedom won

myself, and the balance of life is stressing me out of my mind on what I can do to save my self.

Most days, I express to myself how weak I am, but courage says I am strong when you know your weakness.

You are most "beautiful" when you think of yourself as ugly. As I cry on the reflections of life, I am learning to appreciate my flaws. As I learn my mistakes, I will become one day wiser to stop drinking altogether.

Freedom won

Dear Beloved:

A pleasant and happy rise to you, sister, and queen mother of mine:

I hope this letter reaches you in the best of health because God knows. I feel like I am dying from not recognizing you, my self.

My head is in a spin like the wind had just hit me profoundly, and I cannot flow to breathe once more; please come and free me.

I took a walk in the park today to clear my head; It is -filled with thoughts of Veronica.

As she is in heaven to un suppress my feelings to tell me to drink, so I am walking, and the leaves are fallen off every single tree.

As I walk more, the breeze got me thinking of the smell of the rain as the water pour more -laborious and more cumbersome to hit my cheeks as I continue to walk through the rain.

I am inclined to cry as to being in the elements of I cannot breathe, and I need help.
As I continue my walk, the thoughts of death hit me again.

My eyes are- closed as I am writing you this letter as I envisioned you reading this. I envision you drowning in tears as I need to say, please don't cry.
Please understand today is a tougher day and much even harder for me to get up and put all of my thoughts on paper to you.
I wanted to thank you in advance for reading me with patience and not to judge me as I may be dead when you finish reading me again

I am so sorry, my beloved self, please forgive me.
I hope God takes me in peace as I cannot go through life empty on earth anymore.

Beloved, I have been searching for you for days now, I was wondering if you could just show up because my body is requiring a hug.

Freedom won

Yesterday I wrote myself a suicide letter to say goodbye to myself. God, the thoughts of no one, would ever miss me was not even considered, because I know I wouldn't be missed by anyone.

My days of living are coming to a close.
As- I am planning how to end me. And go out peacefully in my sleep.

I hope you will forever forgive me because I got so tired of my existence without meaning, that I must go, about two weeks ago Veronica came back and ruined me.

As I struggle with her on the inside of me. It is as if she created a file for me to my death.
So I cheated on myself and him, I when looking for what not to expect now I am here wondering out of my mind if she will come out again and do worse, so please help me die.

I am drinking more than I ever did before.
I had the pleasure of making myself some Texas tea this morning with a peach Lipton tea bag and some cough syrup and vodka to numb me as I cannot bear life.

Please go ahead and judge me beloved because I do need to be judged by you.
I am so tired I when to church on Saturday, and I felt like the pastor was talking about me as if he could -possibly understand my problems, how dear he preach about me, at this damn point.

I am glad I didn't confess my sins to him, because the entire congregation would have known about my depressed state of mind. I cannot make myself love myself.

I am asking you to help me let the ole me out, or if not do you think suicide is still my best option as I cannot breathe most days as the pain mounts upon me each day.

Freedom won

I am still crying, I am a broken vessel with scars to showcase each day I need love, and I need peace of none I have please I cannot dream I cannot breathe as the morning lights out I want to find indeed beloved all I need is hope. But its as if beloved doesn't need me, I cannot cry because I have no tears in me to cry.

My river sprinted out of the water along time ago, so please honour me.

All that I am asking you to do is help me plan my murder and tell no one that I ended my life.

Today is Thursday, so the day would be perfect to end me it is a cold day, and I can cause a fire to pretend I was cooking, and the gas exploded on me and took me out cold; it's a perfect plan.

I am not sure if they would even care to investigate, so we are right again; I am not sure if this is -really me talking or Veronica. But she is killing me daily.

As I am now struggling. To escape her as the daybreak

Please understand, I am premediating on my thoughts as a killer to kill veronica me my self.

I am now back in my own body and my dear beloved. I was so scared out of my mind that Veronica would kill us as the day ends, please don't let me go to sleep because I do think she wants us dead.

I am not sure if this is just a dream?

I do "know" "rest" took you away from "me" beforehand.

As I cannot go through. It all over again now.

As to why the inside of me wants me dead is a question.

I am giving all of me, and I think apart of me wants to live. As I believe I do love you, my self, but the other side of me is still drowning in sin, as I dream of setting me free, I wish you would come to my aid and restore inner peace on the inside of me.

Beloved, please understand I need a miracle and your it, and if your not it, I have departed to my departure to end rain; please run fast enough to catch me as I am flooding away.

"I cannot swim."

Beloved, I am now ashes, please take care.

Freedom won

A written Message:
"Journaling" into the entry of grace, I am at peace with myself.

As many think of peace

As a purchase to pay for, I think of order as my livestock to holding on to forever.
My tag line, " I am not my mother as I will offer worth to myself; she will see my values; I am not just her daughter; I am a mother."
As a child of God, she is "undoubtedly" not mines to hold onto because I was thought of by God and given birth to through her as a reward to feel and breathe pain to testify that I am his beloved.

Last year this time, I was on a level to medicate while lending grace a helping hand into my inner peace of mind.

At each turn, I realize I wasn't walking alone; I had God leading me into the balance of change and forgiveness, yes.

Many days as I was at my low, I sorted grace to tell me not to drink or slut my thighs again, as many didn't know my pain.
I was afraid to- tell many things as I am now like open-air to oxygen and breeze. I fear nothing but the death of my flesh.

To deliverance- my God gave me a purpose for myself.

As awake. And a pick me up into my "Purpose" again to increase my rise into the freedom of my mind.

 As the crossroad holds many intersections to a crossing guard wearing yellow reflectors to my caution.

Freedom won

I am no longer numb by hurt, and I hope I will soon become unnumbed by what we all cannot change. As a nation, we shall rise, yes, but as black as we are most days, it too feels like there is no one nation under God because the error is not corrected.

As many humans states they run the lights of red when it's on danger, I often wonder what happened to green and yellow on safe, as I am now within my time, and unclean I am away from him. So, to hear another queen and king speak of running the red light not on green but polluted, I am bothered, because even lions and cows escaped the touch of a male in their season of dirty.

 The thoughts of hearing it, again and again, I am now asking the question, why would you have sex on your blood?

The stain that corrupts the essence of pain and drips stain and the same spirit infused in a pad to a bloody bag while the soul leaves a scent.

Their thoughts of what we do as most are -truly. Sickening as we call it a pleasure.

 I am a hypocrite is a question as I reflected on the subject matter in question again, I have now concluded I wouldn't have because I am in unsafe and nothing clean.

As a student, I am always in teachings of what God is offering as a child. I will never stop attending classes because I cannot ever stop being in the training of what I must study to surpass by the graded mind, and so, shall I be ready to sit and listen to learn a master lesson?

Too often we wonder about what happened to us-
The truth is today; you need to tell yourself all you want to do is "live."

Man to now thinks about how precious my mind is. As an archive to my body, it stores data and recycles all of our many pain. But today is the day to tell it to let me replace all of that with beloved. Just think about how happy you would be.

Freedom won

Why do I pray, because I am not only praying to myself, and for only myself but an uprise?.
As it's known to man, we are all spirits with this body that he flows through daily.

We are so much like the main water stream for right now until the water commission says we have no more water in us.
It's a drought, the deficiency to not produce is a pain honestly — Just to think that the water is a God that runs through you, and nothing will change the love he has for you to stop running on a daily-

We need to improve on our methods with life as we grow. We will learn we cannot preserve ourselves; there is something greater keeping us God.

Freedom won

Today is Friday the thirteen dawnings of a full moon and the day after a well celebrated new years in Ethiopian fashion.

As I am happy to see life again.

As I converse with my brother. As I encourage him to pray more and daily to God, our creator because he has been so good to us.

Lesson into sin:

The process to progress is a sin of yesterday, as Saturday was the last day since my own body touched the water, and my skin felt lotion again, and my tooth came to know paste.

The thoughts of my body are in the smell of the devil as the same flames of burning urine to my piss should kill me because I have not entered the water to my mouth. Again is another sin to find beloved because here I was still giving values to what wasn't worthy of me.

As the day should come to light, Monday was here. And I was no different as Tuesday. I turned on the showers to feel the water and brush my teeth again.

As I was in disbelief of all my. Pain, where it hurts, is nothing. Because I am still not free as I will exchange words back with him as to why I don't know.

Freedom won

The Duration of A Double Revelation.

The sadness of flesh is the same as the power you crave it each day and moment of what you want to infuse anger and rage as I was upset by madness; I became disobedient.

Most days, I am a confusion with the façade of a folly to think of.
My pain and the facts of my sin with my incest body of a thing call flesh.

I use the excuses of a thought I had, and we disrespected God in the middle of a hotel.
I became his whore as it wasn't our first time the sin of drunken captured us, and we became one to exchange broken.
Like a scar that left us fighting and within hate for each other, the question was to be asked.
As we told ourselves not to ever talk about it, and we never did until I had arrived in the house of God to worship, as the essence of broken and beaten had me.

I was praying away the presence of God not to open me up like a bottle to drink as he took me back to each night, and each time we spend giving ourselves to each other.
As the beaten of pain entered my heart, I was in a cry to ask him not to let me speak, but I was no match for him, as he had me like a cord, and I twisted me away, and I was popped open.
In the middle of a church, I made my first confession, as it wasn't my first time.
I then came to realize that my body was like my ancestors, and I was in the midst of a recycled circle call, hostage and bounded as I let God in, it was the more I see. I was like an assassin with my vagina to each water of saliva as it was now spring, the last tongue was my grave, I am grace as peace needed me I am in the presence of repent as a regret came upon me to see I am at home now.
I am not sure how I got to what was once was.

But the truth is I am happy to be free.
To one is a real essence of peace as I would never have made it without him by myself, I will never question his age.

Freedom won

I am in the element to ask the question of him that. I needed an answer from the start of the 1700s. My family was -enslaved, and now I am in the Twenty-first century to ask him why the upgrade to slavery? But with a bit more of what man would call class, as the system breaks me to attract myself to defeat and pain of what is.

Like one day, I was in the house of God, and all that was in my head as I was praying was his name and my mistake never to tell. But I think she knew what we did as well as she later hated me and wanted to poison me for a crime of my madness and flesh of failure.

I wasn't in the right space of mind to have committed actions of sin. As I would dwell on him, so did I stay on her to taste, God how broken I was a (statement) as I pray for forgiveness of my sin.

I now accept Jesus Christ as my personal "Lord" and saviour. Son to man as I am not worthy.

I pray for the rain of glory to change me as I have sinned against myself and you lord, I am genuinely sorry.
Know I was- molested. And taken advantage of raped and mistreated, as I remember crossing the roads of pain, he laid me on my back on the floor and entered me many nights.
I know him as I now see his face, not in my dream but a reality to know he hurt me all in one as my head is a vase broken into pieces, I am not talking out audibly but in silence, as I have a secret.

Freedom won

Psalms:

Psalms is a book that has all the medicine to many scriptures as I read away in the elements of pleading my cause, oh lord I am in the middle of stolen and broken salvation is my new fate and faith is my new enemy to pray, so I am in a scripture.

So, my mind is in blessed is my transgressions, is forgiven as the nest has passed by me so many times, I am at a loss for words.
Here I was in rejoice as sin carried me in pain to relive.
As the day of noises sings in my head, here was beloved saying I will bless the Lord at all times his praise shall continually be in my mouth.

In the book of the Psalms, I find all of me my pain and same as a victim of many things I am so in a shell fragile to break, so I cry out to God as I know. Man as changed many of his words into their own. I am still finding him in me and all things in him because what man has erased, I am now finding when I am in the meditations of him.

Freedom won

Genesis:

Each day I walk a more extended walk because life is nothing of what I planned for it to be.

Most days, I am not myself as the rain poured down on me as I am in a cave asleep and damp wet with no covers to shield me from all I feel inside and out, and it is okay because I am not afraid of the cold no longer or anymore.

As I am finding the lessons to lessen my pain, I see him again up close and personal, looking into my eyes.

As the pain of what was taking me in and reflecting grace didn't serve me wine or a drink of water to quench all of my pain yearnings, I am still at a standstill looking for God to carry me home out of this body I no longer need.

I am running out of options as the rain is still pouring, I cannot feel the water because I am numbed by all I am feeling.

It's written that people's files are not their work but how do you justify my pain, because it's my file and I am my work.

As I got into the beginning of this. Nothing is -written with what I have to the rights of my self.

I woke up knowing everything about the day was not right as I cry for grace to save me and deliver me as I was still dwelling on the façade of what I had created as it hits me here come genesis all over.

Like genesis, nothing I have envisioned for myself is the same as I dream in purpose, I am walking with a cause to change. My fore-parents before me were curious as am I to reflect "Genesis" and understand why I am still yet not free.

I am not in chains, of by literal, but I am in the bondage of all I have endured with the un methods of freedom of which I have none still, yes I have made peace with myself as many things always keep me in a place of rage and unwilling to try.

Freedom won

My mother wasn't my best friend, nor was I mine myself; I was at my low after every visit to pain and hurt.

A prayer to self —

Lord, I am in the middle of the rain as I am wet from water, you are my shelter from the storm.

Last year into this year, as I was praying, I told myself I wanted to give all of me to you as I will render all my heart and soul- to you, God.

I Had this tagline to tell myself I am not my mother as I feel her pain in all I was facing, I had to reconnect.
I am praying, and I am praying-
I am not afraid as the sun sets in the skies each day and week into nightfall; I am as dark as the Phoenix to rise and raise power so that I will pray.
Have you ever envisioned yourself? As a box too heavy to pick up? But when you get to the surface.
You are as empty as a shell. Nothing on the inside of you to hold on to?
I had to pray all a that away from my soul to no longer hold on to it, the powers of God's love for me is a blessing, the confusion of life to live kept me in bondage.

Most days I am so much more like my mother a prediction from birth and an imperfection raising myself to stand alone, the sea as so much water in it that is me a river running to a stream of freedom, where my point of destination is alone to rise in shame and pain.

The medicine

All, I ever wanted was to be is free but I am not so I am at the acceptance of pain nothing is the same the thoughts of hurt is me as I clothed my back from naked I reflect my heart all in the same methods, of change grace and home to save me from it all.
Somedays, I want my ex to want me all in the same, but then again, I don't want the same things he wants from me, which is a façade of life to use me.

Freedom won

Month to Date :
January -2019

The pain we feel is unbearable, as well as the secrets we carry inside of us.

The closure is nothing if you cannot tell the truth about closure and what it does to you on "a" whole as a person.

I wrote to me - myself to help me, and I am not sure if I wanted to let go of what was going on in my head.

April was one of the most trying times as I did everything I could to put Her Raw Burden out I got all "know," and promises, my upsets were with a lot of persons that didn't understand my pain and couldn't imagine what my scarring was doing to me as a person as I took all know.

I now realize my war wasn't with them because God was prepping me for something greater.

As I wrote "her" and I had gotten to the original version edited, but it wasn't my truth nor my pain; it was more like a recreation of what I didn't understand.

So, as I cried to a person stating to me if you don't like what I did, you can change it because it's your work, my God, as I looked over at the file.

I deleted it all and said never mind I don't need to write this book anyway, two weeks later into a state I was prompted by grace to don't give up and just type so I did. Away I when as I was writing I was editing then I got to a place where I expressed to me if I had ever seen a beauty mark, I replied with a yes as it stated they don't ever go away no matter how much polishing you do the blemishes still remains.

Freedom won

So, I got to thinking why should I filter my pain nor chapter my hurting as I wrote me and all that was in my heart, I was now in a better way with my true self as I got started it was like I was talking to God as I write me away.

As May now enter my presence. I was getting ready to launch my eBook as many had it to say and look like what is this mess as I watch them through my Insta stories hiding behind the mirrors and walls to gossip as they judged my writing.

I had to reevaluate my thinking, and everything I was thinking of how cold many was as some pretended to care like my in corrections and non-correcting habits wasn't a bother to them.

As they couldn't read my Farrin language of what I typed up as my English language wasn't adequate -enough, in other words, unreadable, As I listened.

I didn't care because that was me, a person that didn't want to be edited. I was myself and truth as well as unpolished by what I knew was right in my heart, like who has time for stopping to capitalizing on pain.
When Jesus just carried across to be nailed to it, they didn't even want him to have a break, so why and what made you think my mind was in the "error" and yes, not an era to correct anything.

Other than I was having a conversation with me. My self and was relating all the hurt there is in the world to feel as time got closer.

I pressed publish and unpublish to correct to incorrect again with typos as I was happy I got everything off my chest I was unbothered by views because I didn't hide behind anyone or screen and talk rubbish and let it out.

Freedom won

Welcome to my journal again I am un-chaptered

My name is Alecia Smith:
I am myself, and different I don't want to allow the methods of others
to define me as I type in my head.

 I will sit and binge write- myself away and edit nothing because God is
not a modified version of self and flow; he is the I am and the
beginning he created knowledge as he did the power of which he as
given me to write.

So as I write me away I am hoping for all things.
All and most books I read are- chaptered.

 But life and creation weren't chaptered nor numbered; you just know
the starting time of life was in the beginning, and all things are- brought
to an end.

Death is "pre-estimated" by body heat, and the temperature it's not
chaptered but, however. Recorded, then set dates to burials, as you plan
in your head service to preach.

God may have a different PLAN for you to deliver a function, so don't
chapter what you cannot and will not understand is subjected to a
change.

Freedom won

The end gain:

Pain is not just optional; it hurts really bad, as well as it puts you in a place you don't want to be in; each day. I am surrounded by takers and breakers.

Waking up yesterday knowing I reported all of the pain was a reality check for me as many will be asking many questions; most days I wondered if I wanted to answer-
A few weeks ago, my ex and I started talking again; it was all innocent until all I would find myself doing was reflecting on my past pain. Each day it got stronger as he continues to hurt me in many ways than one.

Weeks into talking, I guess as humans, we all do become foolish things as to why we sometimes still love the people that want to hurt us. I saw this quote stating, don't sin, by letting anger control you. As I reflect, we are all sins, and sinners, nothing shall change that no amount of water.

As we cannot understand ourselves and the methods of when we should stop and maybe don't sacrifice being valuable just to be relevant and visible to people that don't appreciate us.

The end of my pain. And the findings .of my beginnings to a start over freedom is everlasting to heal.

As to why the disclosures of the same word as my revelation will still expose me, I am not sure if it is because I am walking and not running was questioned by myself?

I know that anything that will cost me my peace of mind is way too expensive for me to purchase, knowing I cannot return my happiness

Freedom won

for the madness that I got charged for, so I am settling in my silence of letting my peace reign.

The thoughts of how I (right) is not clear to many yes and it's ok as I am myself, I don't expect you to understand me.

Often times, I wonder how does it feel to ask someone to read me while I am standing in the middle of that conversation with no manuals to guide us just read away. As I am "righting," I am searching for all my writes to find beloved. As God is grace, I know I am covered under the blood.

I opened up my book, and immediately, I am in my head with nothing but thoughts. As I expressed in her, I want nothing more than to help little girls; as I hear stories, one out of every household is a victim of rape are have been molested in a home by someone they know.

I don't care to reference if I am using has or as or there and "their" correct, because my ancestors didn't edit themselves, they acknowledged that they were slaves enslaved by others.
Knowing when the break came, they were free full stop "periodt" write not a dot they didn't understand, and maybe I am crazy or mad as many states I don't care.
Spending quality time with oneself is essential as you journey to become, so shall I journal the error to be? As many ask the question of why error and not era as I cannot express my in corrections, I guess I am chosen to right differently.

As I am in the land of all things to gain and excel beyond what I -was given, I know I am free to see and become.

What got me here and freed me was hearing others crying for what they had endured becoming as I "cry" about the same methods to change myself.

Freedom won

As I lose my mind to gain, I promise to change all I can with clean drinking water because we need gallons of clear to survive and flush away what we don't need to kill them inside of us.

Freedom won

I am free:

I am free
I am a production of my beliefs in grace had me.
Yes, to rise everlastingly with grace.
I am free
I am not running I am walking freed by grace.
I am selflessly sharing my pain to heal another.
I am free
I am free
As I dream of infecting others with grace, and the finding of hope lies
in all of us to change and inspire.

Freedom won

Infectious:
Thy weapon is a curse.

The thoughts of a lie you keep on telling yourself that your smile is contagious as everything in life.

As you are quarantined to life damn if you do damn if you don't like death is still at your door.

Realizing you have been stupid to many things, and life had you wondering if you had made all the right choices.

How can you love a man that doesn't love you is a question and a problem all at the same time?

You learn to stop and let it go and move on from it as it's a lesson well learned.

I have done all I can do to inherit this pain and move on from it as a choice never to let this happen to me again in life.

Today I was expressing myself, and last night, I was crying broken and in tears of what I cannot change.

As he as shamed my heart with all his lies, I was no different from him as I loved a fool and by disaster to end me, he is the CD I never want to play ever again.
Now is the question as to where do I stand in his life?

As I call on movements of moments to no answer, I now know the trilogy wasn't real.

As I was so wrong to love him as I have placed my lips upon his lips of which I never do, the explicit of the content of me needing

Freedom won

to cuss is killing me. As I cannot express, what happened last night on Nov 9 and inbetween 1:00 am as we fought through the night of what a night we had, into the morning, he said nothing to me, again after more calls still nothing, so I did the one thing Lisa now would do I slept next to him.

As I felt the pressure of his cock on me and a hug, I was about to give myself to Eric as this wasn't a dream I am now awake to get up and walk away.

Freedom won

The ending of 2018 and the starting of 2019-

"One of my many spiritual philosophies is that to whom much is given so much more- is expected of.'

Spirituality is beyond you and is very much hard to understand if you didn't take away anything from creation and what generations of our people had to endureth to change and be freed by.

Knowing God is the most powerful essence of life, and still, we were in bondage of what he created is a shame, but again, we have nothing that belongs in the same light because we have ruined change chance and being.

In the beginning, he created all things of beauty, of which he hasn't stopped, but it's being -destroyed. By poisoned mind states of curious and disobedience yes and heroes who say there are playing God.
 The diplomacy that divides me and my blackness, but oh, I am viewed to be caramel. Or light-skinned as they would state by the thinkings of society.
I am my activator to elevate and motivate my self as I grew, I see the world, and by knowing and understanding inner peace.
I am a question yes awaiting an answer, as many looks at me differently to question my pain; I am still moving away from them to achieve-

We are from the dust, so it's written, but I don't see us exploding and bursting out into the elements of sand when we die; instead, we rot and become compost now to the new age fertilizer to make organic compound and make the soil better.

As to why man is still using us as test subjects. I have no idea, so my beliefs in the ending of my retired body are to be transcended into the elements of fire, and surpassed the seas overlooking outdid the same word, yes, all in one exceed this life through all things that are the earth.

Freedom won

Wowed by the thoughts of distance and pain is everything. And nothing at the same time to balance.

As each progress to see and achieve. We still drown in the midst into the middle of all our dreams. As a middle child by my parents, I carry all things of burden.

As my mother left me home to be responsible, and I grew to pain. She never asked if I was okay with mothering my brother's as cleaning house was my chores to do each day, so did washing cooking and cleaning became a job without pay.

The prestige notion of hate and love all in one is respected by what I and many think is fear. As I am still in the elements of if it wasn't for me, it wasn't- meant to be.

Stature as given me nothing as its to build I cannot see what I have figure other than pain and disappointments by all and who I have trusted to let be freed by my soul, but my body was enslaved and use to mistreat me my self.

As I have cried many days, I am still in the same crying state enriched by power and knowledge to release all my scars.
As I am- set to win through at as broken, my patience is not my name and cause.

Freedom won

The thoughts:

Have you ever thought about giving up, well don't?
Nothing in life is easy.
Yes, we all know that, but think about the love you uphold from God,
it's beyond here.
He is not away from you; he is on the inside of you.

Dearing you to win and try, he is that intuition saying you must try.
Even when things are breaking you, and you're at the end of the rope to
hang yourself.

Just call on the inside of you and tap in and call on him because no
man can roll thunder nor strike lightning, so let him in and breathe for
the day.
I am unfiltered living in grace and not worried about my enemies.
I am as rotten as yesterday and still stinks into today as I cannot
understand my why's of how a thought could hurt me.

As I remember telling him, I love him. As there is a God in "me," it
wasn't lusting; it is pure love.

As I was inclined to listen to another woman talked about the man.
I was in love with as I hear the sound of pain on the inside of me.
I was in silence to don't speak, but listen as my thoughts continued in
my head, she turns on the radio to play.

She is in love with another man by Jasmine, has "she" talks about
him, and how much she doesn't want him in the way he wants her.

I felt broken as I counted all the men I came across, and still, none was
like him as he shines so bright, and I would hate to dim his light.

So I was letting go as I told Karl in my head to go and phuck himself,
and he was one less body to think about. As I have murdered many, I
didn't kill him in my head. But he was still dead to me as I told him to
go to hell.

Freedom won

The day ended with her planning to see her current lover, and still, she was on the phone with him in a "DM."
He is the side toy and a fool he doesn't know that she doesn't want him, as she is in love with her beloved John doe but what the hell, phuck him and his skinny ass, as I call him again still I was going to voicemail as I was now blocked.

I'm in a stressful sort, as the next day I was "provoked" again, as she talks about him still, but it was alright because by now I got it he wasn't for me.

As he had taken the liberty of ignoring all my calls, and we haven't spoken in days, so I got it he wasn't into me, and I was the only one that was fighting for something to call love at first sight.

As I told him to kiss my ass and dropped off the grit, without words, we still haven't spoken in about ten days now to date.
As I strolled past him as he was non-existent to me.

Bodies.

As the talks continue to express the number of bodies she had on her, and he would be her last, I was lost at sea because I was trying to understand what the hell she was talking about.

The conversation with another:

Oh my God, I am now approaching 40, and people justify their sex partners as body counts. I looked at myself and asked my mind, bitch, what is your count with tongues you had entered you, God, I was at 48 and two away from fifty, and I said my vagina is genuinely a burial ground for saliva my God so many tongues.

As I was praying, I dreaded fifty as I had a date on Saturday with a Brazilian beauty. I wasn't going to ask her to eat my box as they call it and make her my 49th tongue. I should be ashamed of being God's sirens to my vagina.

Freedom won

I need a refund and an exchange for the stretching of all dem tongues that like to speak languages to my kitty and now then puss.

As I dwell on many things, I can only think about it. My pain and all the damage to my thoughts of how.
I could allow myself to subscribe to sitting and listening to another woman telling me she has a large unit with nothing. But skeletons in it and to accurately state she got started at age eleven and was pregnant by 15 years of age.

I was like shit this is a testimony as I dear not to judge her because I was going home to drink myself away to vodka if the night were fitting I would even blaze a spliff and call it a night.

Freedom won

July 13th into the 14th
Inner Truth:

I am drinking again, and I am not sure as to why, but I had a few drinks into the darn of night entering into the eve of the morning.
As I drank, I became open to talk about my pain, life, and the thing call sex again.

The conversation of God and his presence surfaces in my mind as to why I am here paying it forward and going through life in the manner I am going through it with as I cry most days for a change.

I am still drinking wine and crying about all my pain, as I have to express all that is in me.
I know I am free as it was -written I am from clay, but my pain hurts like fire and runs like water each day.

My dust is dirty from my wet, and my scene is from being taken too early. As I am no longer ashamed by all that happened to me most days, I am bothered by it all.

The happiest moment I took on in light of disgrace, doors closed windows at a seal, floors crackling and music to a sound silence to a plug of my ears.

As my earphones were on mutation in the sound of transition and an in the entrance to power, many things were happening at once, discovery, history, and geography as chemistry starks steam and lusted flesh and wondering eyes amounted into wanting.

As love as no light but beloved as a whole to render the same methods of love again.

The thoughts of memories appear in dreams and service of what we cannot change as love as no bearings to my heart, but shame knows my sin, and sin knows my shame.

Freedom won

The truth about a lie is dishonesty yes, we all know that I am not here for you. I am here for the "truth."

Many questions to ask, gosh, I wish I had all the rest of the answers. Why I am alive, I don't know, but what I do know. Is that I exist because of chance and change and the option to think I am equal to stand even if there is no rain left in the sky, only drops of dust from my burning ashes after I am gone.

Now ask me where I went to," and I will tell you underground to suffer my suppression of pain and hurt.

I became overwhelmed by pain, knowing that pain doesn't have a Colour but a look of in hurt and a feeling of I am drowning.

As a patient sick in the elements of. My then state of mind.
I have tried just about everything of freeing myself as I cry often, and daily, nothing was changing as grace was from God's pain was from my sin and why he couldn't save me, and my innocence was a question as I hurt each day.

Confirmation

Thoughts to affirm that we don't know what to feel other than pain.
I rise to forgive each moment because I cannot change them; I am not making a big deal out of what I cannot "Change" nor ever understand.

Into a thing call my affirmation:

The inner circle of truth and lies had us and made us each day, God, if you were me, that was told when you accept God as your personal Lord and saviour all your sins will be washed away.

So, I when to the church for them to hear me as nothing was said only welcome has, I sat with my pain in the same place.

Today is June 25th, as I was in the middle of a conversation with my ex shells.

Freedom won

I realize I too have hurt him deeply, as I told him of my pain and what I did to suppress and turn off what no one knew "of" I am still on the watch to suicide, as the sounds of music keeps me I am not yet at one with her.

Writing her was to stop hurting, each bruising was my entry into I wanted a man that would beat me daily, as I cannot express and explain how foolish I was to think it was ok to have those thoughts in my own head

My name is still Alecia today as I can promise you as a woman a man that batter and bruise you is not your friend or your lover, nor does he love you; your only an idea to him and a beating bag, because he thinks you don't deserve better.

Today I understand my worth like no other, as I am now at peace and not in pieces.

Each day my heart is in a better place to change, I want to do nothing but inspire others to change the world we are in and living in.

As I am happy, I found peace to rebuild one of many relationships that means the world to me, and I aimed to work out things with my mother, my queen, my rock. She is everything to me. As I became a mother myself, I now know her pain as she had no manual to raise us as a teenage mom, plus did a great job.

My mother knew that peace of mind wasn't the absence of trouble; it was her path to walk because she didn't have a mother to teach her differently.

Yesterday I had to ask reborn to emerge like nothing to lose but a choice to stand to win as I was in the middle of grace and prayer, I asked of myself never to lose hope in myself nor think less of me.

I was aware that if I didn't heal from the pain, it wouldn't stop because I left it unattended and wounded to carry and feel.

Freedom won

As I reflect on her, I knew that I came up from a real thing call gutter, as I don't want to reveal I must.

I fall in to love as lust had my sin was my capture as I live in it; I didn't escape.

10 14.
My current state of mind.
I was embarrassed and out of MY mind about why I am here in this damn hospital nursing a wound that I had from a slip and fall due to sexual pleasures and accommodating my other self-Veronica.

The thoughts of me not just only being here for my foot was a problem. As I asked the doctor to treat me for any following sickness or STD's even though my results were negative, it was still a problem. I wanted to be okay I had the nurse told me to turn on my right side where she stuck a large needle on the right side of my ass while she lectures me on how painful it is. And it will hurt for a few days. Sick I was highly upset as to why Veronica did me an injustice to slut my thighs without asking, as I was in the thinking of Veronica I wanted to end her life, but I had to think I couldn't have "ended" her without concluding me my self.

As the night continues with me in pain I knew I was wrong to put myself in that space of thought, but it was way too late for me as I cry on the inside of me I knew I couldn't get me back nor would anyone understand my pain.
On a scale of 1 to 10, I am in a flash to drown all over again. Because I am still hurting. As nothing will erase the damage and the hurt of what I did, the more I lie to myself is, the more the pain hurts. As again, I was in the racing of tracing the thing call tongue.

Freedom won

Recap
My Vagina As Embarrassed Me:

I cannot express my addictions to actions. I was on the inside of me for so long.

The plumber was my last lesson for years, AND like an addict, I couldn't kick my habits. Ole ones that wouldn't and couldn't die no matter how long I stayed away from her Veronica.

I was not convinced that one is genuinely into sex, and one Is addicted to oral pleasures.

Her self is nothing but pure confusion. The truth is Alecia hates penetration, so what the hell. Alecia is not a freak, but God's good grace Veronica is a villain to society

The thoughts of when it got started with me being in an addicted state of mind to oral stimulation got started back in 2000 after getting it done maybe a year again it got terrible in 2001, and then I slowed down in 2002 because I was with someone that I truly loved.

-

2003 was both a good and bad year for me, so it got started up again, where I then met my ego, Veronica, she wasn't bad, but she was something else.

2004 she was out, and I had a few relationships, then she was locked up again then back out in 2006 and was in for years until 2008 that was when she came back out again.

I ended things with Eric and was trying to do me as I was not worried about one thing, but I was free. That is when I met Dwayne, and he was the maddest thing on two feet with a tongue of pure heaven.

Freedom won

We never had any form of intercourse he would just orally stimulate me, we lasted for a few months until he wanted more, so we ended things.

During that summer, my friend Kevin would pleasure me. With The same oral stimulation and absolutely no sex other than "oral we ended things due to my selfishness, then it was Cliff and me for years until we stopped and picked it up again to continue or arrangement.

2009 I was back with Eric, and by 2011 we were welcoming our son; we were struggling to stay together. But Veronica would then call Cliff and end things with Eric we would then be "cool" as early 2013 I "welcome" another baby and Veronica was sleeping again. Why I named her Veronica it was more comfortable since my middle name was fitting, I gave it to her.

2015 or 2016, she was back for about a week during football season and when hunting oral stimulations. She then met the plumber that she would go to him to satisfy her cravens; his tongue is everything "she" rated him has a double 30 and was the best she ever had in the world of oral stimulation other than Leslie; she was a beast on two feet.

That was the last time I saw her because I started to suppress her. Within all the spiritual consciousness of life and was changing and evolving for all—the better reasons In life.

As life was okay until a relapse of being home alone, drinking one drink was to fix me from my cold and then.
I couldn't stop whether it was phone cheating or text cheating.
Veronica was- invested as she was in contact with her ex Sheldon and knowing Veronica she was really for Sheldon.
-
Veronica knows Sheldon really well because he entered her world with what she was into so the kill would be a necessary one.
Alecia wasn't interested in him like Veronica so that Alecia couldn't call nor text, but Veronica would when she was under the influence.

Freedom won

She needed him, and he was her game; she doesn't want anything to really do with him but that.

Alecia had urges as she was into Roy and what they could get started on, but Veronica had other plans.

As she ended a phone call with Roy and called it a night, she took a bath, and went looking for a fix like a person on crack on a tree, she founded a goal pot and was ready to prey.

Then the night out with my mentor and Sheldon happen with Veronica headlining the scene of two kills in one night.

Now Alecia as to live with her actions and madness of what she is on. Sheldon was like a vampire to my vagina.

God, my kitty cat, needed a wash and required treatment, because of the amount of saliva he left in me God can one person tongue be so evil, to lick out my entire vagina and "left" nothing in it for the next prey.

He did a full two hours without a break and thought of me to think of calling him again to whore me with his tongue. Still, he was top of my list for 2020 if Veronica was ever to come back out again.

Sheldon was a liar with his lips about being a virgin when I lifted up my legs and told him to feast on me like a beast. He was acting like a virgin, but when he did this thing with a slayer of his tongue, he woke up Veronica to choke him with her legs as she suffocated him with the release of the dragon and held his head to no movement.

He then continues to choke her as her safe word is God he now knows to stop and break, but she cried out, and he continued to lick her as her own body gave out and told him to lets drive and keep my panties as she entered his bed to a lesson.

Freedom won

Three times in one night with him, he made her come as no other man did ever in life as she told him to let me give you a piece of me. For five minutes, she entertained his cock and then his tongue again, then pull a Veronica to argue as she watches him beat his dick with his own hands to release himself because she wasn't going to let him really phuck her. Still, God he was 100 out of 100, I could do time for his tongue if I was ever is lady. But I am not that into him, remember I was the one that called him to service me for a craven of Veronica.

My body is over itself as I will go and attend church to confess again in silence to my damn self of what a sinner I am.
Veronica has finally killed me and disgraced me with more sin to confess on and about with my self why it is a question that needs an answer.

10 .10
I don't think I would ever imagine being strange, but God to know I am different is a problem to my self as I am within the heavens of myself I am crying for grace.

We all live within our thoughts are the state of mind.
Today I have fallen like a soldier in a battle there is no coming back from my scars the markings will always be there whether you want it or not you welcome it.
This is a lesson.
Self-educating my mind as its ahead of me. If you are reading this, I have come to discover my mind as killed me in thoughts of what it wanted, and I took another turn instead.

Noting that I wanted to blame my thoughts of a condition call depression, but the truth is that I am reborn, but the essence of my pain still lives within me as a shame, and that person is all in one and even me.
The truth is it is good and evil within the elements of all of us-
I have discovered my devilish side as she is me, my own self, the lover of poison the thing called a bottle.

Freedom won

A flashback to my week as I discovered I was having an episode of pain, more like a break down as I was mostly alone, the walls came in on me, and I enable pain pills and alcohol to tell my story.
I do believe that by now. I am going mad and out of my way to get back to myself.

As I don't want to ever lie to myself of what the reality of what my truth Is. But As there is a God in me.

I should be happy with what I have. But deep down on the inside of me. I wanted to find me my own self in pain.

As I become what I couldn't manage. Nor handle in my state of consciousness.

As I really outdid myself and discover people are not indeed your friends, they just like a story to have.

Friday into what I did will cause us everything, but as I look at it, I deserve all that pain as a lesson itself, I was the cause of that pain. As I spend hours of the morning nursing my leg and looking for a therapist, I realize I am truly alone in pain with my feelings.

  Many only want a story to look at and ask what happen, but they don't honestly see your condition. Many don't care about what you feel. The day is Monday, as I will give myself a lecture on what I am and how I could not think of what I was doing.

Sunday, I was in so much pain, but I knew what I did to earn my condition is in ways my sentence to my own death as I was the one that killed myself from danger. I am not upset at the world, only myself. I am not as dirty as I continue to desire madness. Or "dirty" at all but, the thoughts of what I like as Veronica is a weapon to hell.

Freedom won

The thoughts of desires:

I was up in the early morning "Eve" as my body was in what they call heath and no flash.

- My thoughts were in lusting as I laid my body down and became a subject to sexually pleasuring my own self. While I think about his device of a thing call cock, God, I know its wrong, to have a love for your friend, but as I tease many others, I only have eyes for him, I want him to enter me in ways of sin and pleasure as I am still scared to the covering of my head I am aware of what I want from him.

> He touches me in ways of no other like a fool I fantasize about him. I text with no replies, so its as if I am talking to myself or telling myself a lie.

I had a moment to make a video of me touching my body and playing with the essence of my kitty cat.

As she wet herself into morning break on a picture of Karl and another, she was inclined to get nasty as she was in danger of another love. It was like Veronica emerged like the emergence from space, and a fairy tale came to past again.

- As I wet myself for Karl as I rang him twice without no answer, my madness had me, so I cry myself to how foolish I was. As I told myself to let go of the smell of his body as being held on to on Wednesday and Thursday, the touch of his hands gave me a release into the morning light as I reflect on goodbye.

-

Now into the eve of the night, Veronica was born again as she was in no mode to ever speak about Karl.

She when shopping, as a friend gave her a call, she picked up not as Alecia. But her twin Veronica the bipolar destruction that walks on two legs, here she was in need of pleasure.

Freedom won

As she only desires one thing. Her addiction of the tongue the slayer of human in thoughts of the spirit, she releases Alecia head covering and become nothing of her as "she" dwells of what a night she is going to have and ruined Alecia, as Alecia is no longer of a sounded mind.

She gives in to Veronica, the devil. As Satan becomes angels, she was in for a treat with the man they call Jean.

The driver, he was older, about 63 years of age as Veronica entertained him and confused his weak mind with words of sin and temptation. She was no saint.

As she continues to remember, she had more tongues in her than a toll stops taking EZ passes. She became an animal again for the hunt as she found a prey as the beast of a lioness arises in her sin and no prayer to freedom.

Veronica was still alive hunting crime.
As she gives in to Jean the driver's tongue, he had her in the back of a car as she had him on his knees feasting like an animal and ushering sounds of out a body experiences.

- Veronica held on to Jean's head and let him eat with his ole tongue as she releases juice of stain on the tip of his tongue.
-
- Then cry for God to save her from Alecia to never come back as she misses the danger of what she was doing years beyond years again if "she should die Veronica was the cause of their death on 9/12 "she" became a drunk again out of her mind.
-
- She cried to herself again as she knew Veronica had done something wrong and out of body.

- As she entered the car. And walked to her apartment.
- She stripped herself naked and threw all her clothes away and took the longest wash of her kitty cat and then anointed it with some olive oil sacred to holy and prayed never to sin again.

Freedom won

Alecia came back to herself and rang Karl, but no answer has she now got the picture of he is not that into you.

- Anesthetics numbed the spiritual essence of her body. She was out of her own body nothing is going to change her from herself ever as she is in sin.

-

- The medicine of madness had her in danger, and her crown as fallen as she is now unholy to sin broken and dropped from the light of life.
- It's now morning dated to 10/13 I just got in from another hunt with Veronica I now remember everything as I am in so much pain due to me running out of the bathroom and falling again to damage my leg once more.
- As he helped me up without much care, I knew I wasn't myself again.
- As I now knew, I had a message on my phone to Roy saying if you read this Veronica is back, and I don't know how to stop her as the morning continues around 4:20 am, I rang Cliff's phone to help save me but no answer.

-

- I now have no thoughts to myself as I will soon recover from her Has the night she had nothing but chokings and plenty of foreplay. Bite marks and swollen thighs bruise marks and headaches with a distaste of madness Veronica was now alone with Alecia to kill her as she woke up from a sleep remembering the night they had two in two.

-

- First, she remembers him the beast that let her scream and bites on the lips of her kitty cat; then, she releases the best perfume in his mouth only to tell him she must run into a meeting.

-

- As she picked up the phone and called the plumber, but he was unavailable to her at that moment so she called the one person she knows that love her and only lies to her as "she" took another it would now be her third, and she was ready for him.

-

Freedom won

- As she asked the beast to service her with his tongue in ways than you could only imagine, he entered her building, and she got into his vehicle. As she stated to him, we are not going far, so he turned into the parking lot of two buildings over and pulled up the seat as Veronica climbed into. The back of the car he then got out and entered the "back" with her as she put on a Dexter daps and was no longer in her black thong panties as he kneeled on his knees and held on to her throat and choke her, her feet "was" in the air as she cried out baptize me in the back of the car and noise was her best friend.
- I now realize what I did last night, and nothing will change the pain as I call myself hurt.
-

Freedom won

I trust the pain, and the pain betrayed me in the end to lose as I will win, I am still missing-

As I was planning a wedding, to a man that I knew didn't really want me because he loves me, but because he was planning on taking me to the cleaners, as a punishment for leaving him, it's funny how he didn't change he is still the same.

I should listen to my mother as the pain gets to be unbearable and stressful; all I did each night was sob.

I am now distant in time to try and recreate hope as I am a barren to my own ovaries, I will need a carrier to have the remaining of my children as I will resurrect dream again in the light.
As I am consciously talking to myself, this is not a dream; it is my reality of feeling freedom again.

You will never get to live the same way you have imagined it, but an intelligent life as its own loan to work for you and not how you want it.

The loan to life is an easy cash handling policy that if you abuse it, it gets revoked like a visa issued to you.
So, my loan was a pain, yes, as I carried it, I also cashed it out, God now I am on low and to a penny to choose life over death pain over inner truth, why is my circle of evolvement so burdened by rage?

The inner truth of all of me is that I want to live not on my terms, but whatever plans God had for me to rise and travel into, as I grew, I wasn't looking into yesterday but hoping for tomorrow to one, so I can make a change and see life.

I believe in:
The spirits of life will always exist; your body just needs a new vehicle to drive in as I conditioned my thoughts to trust and fail to rise.

Freedom won

I was in the middle of Sunday, while on Saturday, I was pronounced stupid and Friday I fell to fall in love with the ideas of pain again to relive broken.

As I had asked of my wings to fly. I wasn't blazing anything in my thoughts to create only to live in the same elements again of what I don't understand.
As each day, I meet another that carries pain in their heart hurt like no other.

As I stayed in line with an open mind to think of all I will hear from others what I cannot change is a pain, today is Tuesday my mind state is connected to Thursday as private became open to talking about as I cry with her.

I realized my wounds were healed, but her scars were a burden as a course to "reverse" fail she has no clue to understand the distance of pain with her and mother as her rage grows it pains her to a cry as she only sees hate for her in her eyes.

There is nothing but fear as she sees him loving her, she doesn't know what to do, with herself as her life is lived in her shadows again to be beaten by rage.
The craziest thing I had to tell myself is to stop surrounding myself with my losing streams of running into failing but get up at the root and inform losing I am tired.

As I was determined to change so many things, I had to change me first.
My Mondays are to evaluate me as my Tuesdays are to become my Wednesdays, and my double methods are my determination and all of my Thursdays as I rise to see hope in God's work for my purpose. Fridays are I am going out to show out, and that's Saturday's resurrection, and Sundays healing the minds of thoughts.

Freedom won

The secrets we carry:

Shattered and broken is playing in my head as I reflect to let go. Still, I am shattered, but I am not broken. It is my way to render peace.

As I no longer worried about my troubles because God got me as my secrets are my trials.

I must endure all that I have to take to become, Lord, I am crying, but even though I am "curvature," I am still wounded, with the strength to rise like no other today.

I have "carried" many secrets as I have tried not to remember them, they're driving me into a puddle of mud. As I let go of the fantasy of due justice because deliverance had me to clear my rage as I will rise into the morning high.

Lord, I knew my struggle as there was a curve in the road to reflect on the grass, which wasn't green enough to show me the mud of pain.

You grow to lose your mind into what it should of look past and through. I open me up to the truth because it burdens me and my heart the secrets had me at a hostage point.

The bonds of blood mean nothing because they are not holding us together; it is dividing us because we balance rage and jealousy and betrayals and envy for each other.

What I have is not love in them but the convenience of what I can do for them, so these days I find myself alone like God no matter what I have done for the name of good, there is always something.

Freedom won

Most days, I learn to be alone all by myself as many as only use me to win for themselves and have left me to lose like a battle to a war I wasn't fighting for myself.

As I tell myself that I am- rescued, and I don't need no one else to save me but me.

I cherish today because yesterday is gone, I cannot hold on to it and "dwell" because I cannot change what he did to me.

When I first got started on my path, I didn't know where I was going, but gratitude informed me that kindness is not a sickness; it's a cure and medicine to heal.

As- compassion is not to compare. But to become more significant than anything negative in your path to change and erase.

I used to sit and ask myself, girl; your phone didn't ring today; is everything ok does anyone remember you?

As I have learnt to understand when some don't need you, they will not call because they do not require you at that moment in life as I got older, I told myself to tell what I felt.

As I explained away to let them know your friends who are not, my friend should never know anything about me, or should you share my personal business as to why I am unconsidered by you and then I am done being used.

Freedom won

FATE:
Of a mustard seed.
Fate and Fortune chance

 Providence luck and destiny are all defined by one-word wisdom to become and foresight all things.

 In frugality, yes, look at God's work at how many meanings you can take away from one thing one word and multiply all aspects of your inner being.

I am that of a seed growing again by faith and fate of a belief that he is my purpose, and all I am required to do is love him throughout each day and night.
God, I am no longer afraid to sleep and travel away to my past and the pain to reflect all aspects of my growth.
Faith, the methods of patience, is to stand.
The dysfunctional madness of pain is that no one is coming to save you from your own self.
The thoughts of change are unbalanced. By madness, rage, and shame all over again in reverse to all the why's.
 I am not myself in a dream that is not right.

As I am in the elements of inner truth:
The importance of taking care of my thoughts are upon me because when I am alone, there is no one to help me take care of my words to preserve me from drowning in them. As water is my body, and drowning is still in the elements of water, I cannot swim away from my pain.
I am now in elements to surround myself with dreamers that want to aspire and inspire others to dream. I want to see myself.

What pain cannot buy money gives you to feed the rage of hate.
Learning that you need to love and find true happiness is a must-
Inner peace is a balance.
Integrity is a method and standard to be and must be -upheld.

Freedom won

A quote to my ole soul to relive my blessings each day
"The start of the day is with purpose and rise to hope as I will, only
gain and receive blessings- to overcome."

The reference to worth is that your value is priceless:
Learning that the mental state of your mindset will have no attributions
to your mind.

Once you have learned that the attritions of hate will keep melting you
away, what will you do to stop the abrasion from bleeding you out
from the inside to save beloved?

- love yourself beyond fear
- Count your own happiness
- Inner peace is necessary, so you must lose "to gain."
- Integrity doesn't need to be "complex: nor be compromised.
- Your volume must have base don't ever lack character.
- House is home, so manners are necessary.
- Showing yourself a limit to how your behaviour gives you
  respect
- Don't lose the benefits of what you need to have to gain your
  morals.
- Loyalty equals trust; it is natural to give and receive.
- Virtue rectitudes must need honours, so you must have the
  same meaning to one, which is the morals of things to have
  patience.

Talking points:
The things we all love are the comfort, yes, we are too comfortable
depending, and not understanding sometimes no one is coming to save
us from our own self.

Fashionable, I place too much on myself. As a person to want to achieve
and with that, my bars were set too high.
I fail myself on the counts of not taking by each day and a set at a time
to heal from pain.

Freedom won

- I am not even sure why I was procrastinating on things to achieve, but I viewed not wanting was indeed best for me in the start to go after what I truly wanted in life.
- Why didn't God save me was a question.
- I blame my parents for many of my issues, with men in general and the confusion of why I should want a woman in my bed.
- Self-inflicted pain and unforgiving shames to bearish each day to awake were a "considerable" problem.

Tag line:

The mind can be both an enemy and a friend choosing the right one can sometimes be a problem if you are still in the delay of pain.

Loyalty is like a train; its only concern is speed, and once it as arises at the destination point, it's like you never existed only recorded by miles and will remain in the black box for life.

I dedicate my mind body and soul to the methods of healing. As it is a national month of awareness for my madness- to relieve daily, of course, no one talks about these things.

A "substantial" and tremendous dedication in my milestone to heal my own self the pills and alcohol and cough syrup did nothing to make me better, as I can sit and cry, I ask myself what is next?

Today I rose to dedicate a star to my heart, knowing I have shined beyond the expectations of man and embrace my truth.
Appreciation of thoughts:

To My babies, the day will arise when you must be a part of a change, so know your history.

We are leaders of a tribe to receive the energy of pain, and it's wise that you must heal and make a difference.
I have done my part by walking in my truth.
To my earthly mother, I love you as the sun will set and rise in the sky to reflect the glow of beauty:

Freedom won

To my soil that planted me in purpose by a drop of a specimen, I salute you for helping to produce me.
To my heart, we shall rise as one in hopes of changing together. I salute you.

To my father, the layers of my body and spirit within me, I give you my beloved heart to rescue each day and heal me from breaking. I welcome your presence.

As many times as I look up into the blue skies, I don't know what I was looking for in thin air because God is in me, and he walks with me.
The thoughts to self is I should acknowledge all my achievements yes but, then it requires all matters of degrees of which I have none only the temperature from the sun to "acknowledge" oh boy do forgive me my own self.

I am not sure where I should label myself of schools attended as if that should do me any form of justice to my injustice methods but, nevertheless.

I will attend college this fall and not the dungeon, and I will be majoring in my own thoughts, I guess the terms are psychology these days, I wonder if my professor is fit to do my psych-evaluation?
As I am to madness, I will be writing and editing myself.
As I wake up each morning after I had let the world into my entire life, I realize I wasn't burdened I was free as the daylight in the sky as I cried free me, God, as I am not alone as I walked into freedom.
One of the things I dreaded was my truth as I prayed to tell all my pain, but knew I had to say I too was molested and raped and taken advantage of my God.
I took a note pad the other day to add up all my lovers, and I was ashamed of what my pain helped me become, in the end. Pain won at defeating me before I got to succeed in the end.

Freedom won

Learning-
Another day to discuss.
We cannot carry what will not depart with us.
-Money is temporary earnings that bring us high stress and loss balance.
-House is just a shelter, but if God wants the rain to pour all coverings,
shielding you will disappear.
-A car is just a faster transportation, but it will break down and need
fixing.
The career is temporary.
Trust what is everlasting because God is eternal. The self-beliefs of your
own fate in him bring you places that contain joy.
As I read to myself this:
I invest way too much in others because I want to see the best in them,
but I don't have anyone to tell me they see the best in me.

They only see the ideas I disburse into reality as a lesson to self; I now
speak less as to why I don't trust many is still a question.
Learning pain is my energy and constant stress as I rise to win each day
I am running, with no stop each roundabout I stop at, I am still learning
that I am my mother's daughter.

I have learnt you will find yourself supporting people that don't care
about your vision nor want to give you a day of support, and I am more
in the elements of takers.

I strongly believe in my heart that my positive and infectious energy as
impact many; they just won't say it as to why I don't know, and it's ok
as I only not live for self but for others.
Each day I see many for what they indeed are in the end game of things.

Freedom won

Why?
As I grow

I grew pain, rage, and betrayals as I wrote in my diary in my head, on many of my lessons to ask each day, was I okay, and can God truly save me from myself.

As I express how we can all relate to each other by the thoughts of suicide again, I am still. In the dying transition of a dream to travel back to my pain each day as I cannot face many things awake but in a sound to a "dream" by noise.

As you know, I hate chapters and numberings of my thoughts, my methods to place me on paper is different.

BUT:

To understand that pain is one "powerful" hurt is another pain by itself.

What I have in me is not and is a pain at the same time, to relate to each and every day.

I use all my desires to recreate my rape and what I wanted to release myself from, but at this age and point in time was all a lie, nothing was freeing me.

My mother didn't even know me as her daughter, nor did she know I had gotten raped; it wasn't for her to know what my thinking was now it pains her to see my pain.

As I am in a union with her to love her. We are recreating a mother-daughter "union" of love to enjoy each beyond today.

As I reflect on all I faced in life, what I had envisioned as a walk in the park was a drive to crash all of me as it pains me to cry.

As I rise alone each day, my celibacy was a question as I was in training to release my past. As I mourn my own streams into rivers, God was going to save me because he had given the same tools already to stand as I didn't understand myself I wasn't looking for any more sacrifices.

Freedom won

As I could think of what had me like a kid, I play dolly house and experience rudeness as a woman I played house, and I got burned With a scar to carry and render pay, as a queen Reborn to hope I am releasing all I had to transmit.

Yesterday I reflected on him as I wish I didn't have to, but like any ruler, I had to measure distance length and not time because I cannot erase what broke me I can only release.
There is no more war, only the battle to carry because victory was upon me as I told my past I am my future to date.

Freedom won

Dear madness:

My name-is- Ambitious -Lending Elevation & Commitment, Inner Peace & Appreciation.

My name is Alecia, from my family reference, but I am mostly referred to as Lisa (Losing in Sin Action).
After a special visit to myself and finding the peace to myself, I call myself Yaa (Yearning Appreciation & Access).
I was born to a man and a woman, yes me, birth date unknown to "self."

As each day I am reborn from grace, I am still standing in the rain of God blessings showering me down.

My favourite colour blue with red, I guess, create something, figure it out and tell me is the madness to date me as I added it up and minus; I got the reign to rule purple. I am royal.

Love you from the inside- with the flow of the outside.
As life is the most expensive thing and becomes cheap after a shot of a bullet, let me reintroduce myself after death once more, my name is Yaa.
Giving questions to answer:
1. Did you know I like to write?
2. What is my favourite thing to do?
3. What are some of the struggles?
4. Why do I hate to drink?
5. Why don't I trust many?
6. At what age did I lose my first child
7. Why do I hate sex?
8. Why do I stay to myself?
9. Why most of my friends are male?
10. Why do I cry and can't sleep at night?

My Motto

Freedom won

"I refuse to lose because it's set in stone for me to win. I am to focus on losing, so I run to the infinite for covering my shelter forever, IN HIM I HAVE EVERYTHING".

Giving up was of yesterday today I am marked to fuse success.

Explanation to self:

I was asking myself to customize my madness, so I ask Alecia for a rearrangement; she ignores me as I needed to clear my thoughts. I drank water instead of vodka. At the same time, Lisa rearranges our wire to the brain, and she realized we are indifferent to different.

Learning to pick and choose your battles -was always a topic to discuss: As I watch them treat me with injustice to my blackness and not my qualifications of getting things done. I was falling short because I allowed myself to settle, to what they help me to create in doubt of not knowing better and doing better with myself.

I rise to achieve.

I wrote HER because I was lost in the shadows of falling in too deep, so I rose never to understand but embrace all my happy endings in my own mirror of truth as I reflected on beloved and who she is becoming. In taking is beyond a synopsis it's a holder to a cup to drink from, God I know my worth can I tell you, how many times I have cried myself to a pillow asking how could you hurt me like this and not feel my sorrow breaking as I am your own self and skin.

Freedom won

Shame:

Well, the thoughts of you make me vomit and fear to admit I am a bit ashamed of me; most days, I wondered off to self and slept not be. Shame is a madness to talk about daily- as many wouldn't understand.

I needed to unashamed my madness because I cannot take it anymore, as a child I envision graduating from college now I look in a room. Everyone else has a degree, and all I have is the temperature of shame of not achieving a degree of some kind.

But then again here am I asking if it's too late to go back to school? When you have come to the realization that your life is your most magnificent masterpiece, live for now, and enjoy it later. I am genuinely Letting love be my stands on unconditional love without- ceasing no matter the reason to give let it flow naturally.

Because your heart was already -sacrificed, to the things of life- real love promotes from within you glowing black complexion of the inside you cannot see- but know it's there forever to last- the knowledge you receive from within I dominant to give and lead by. This is indeed just a mere reflection on my pain of 22 years of struggles with drinking in private and depress at bay with myself. I was a teenager when I express pain and hate, I have developed a madness over the years, on adopting the counts on multiple version of myself on a daily, to escape what I couldn't understand. The pain was measured by my rage, as I have come to experience a man placing his hand upon my body and sexually abused me and tormented me from sleep. To bring me to his bed and then wake me up early in the morning to pretend all is well, is a sickness of a predator.

On the reasonings, you have read her raw burden you will note as to why chapters are missing to my pain as I will leave it for another time to express my sorrow.

Freedom won

The ink when dry and the keys stop typing to my heart as I had suffered a break down in the middle, I chose to skip that pain, to reset and return.

Be forgiving, and find understanding to be empathetic, but don't be misled by the weakness of your heart.
"Shame is my captured as I told myself to stop dwell in the disaster of my pain, and stain of my scorn, because something beautiful will be created when the storm is over to my inner peace."
The thoughts to shield was never on the table to grace as to why I don't know, and today was a reality yesterday was my darkness.
"I believe you" " I believe in you" I don't know if I should believe your madness is uncurable.

Me:

I don't think it states I needed any- permission to go mad.

However, I needed to report my madness on a scale with the recommendation of medicine to sane.
The reverse of deeming me to Belview, as she tells me my dosage will make me feel- better to date, and I am rescheduled for a refill like a tracking device.

I track my counts to overdose and refill early- like coverage to a shift I am watching the pharmacist.

Me: God is my light and reflectors to shone me from my darkest day. As I reverse current to reverse the one. Nothing that is still current and use in a double standard to service me.

I woke up telling myself to honour God, and the word, as I ask myself what the word is?
"The discernment of sin is sin on a sophisticated scale of enlightenment to sensitivity- of my pain- so the saints deemed me mad on the judgment to judge me to a free God as sent them to me."
I have been crying to see and feel that love for Many years he is here. My God is real.

Freedom won

"My" emotions bearded my soul, as I ask for my currency to cash and change to hold me near and never let go."
The devil was trying me.

To get to me, as he states that he doesn't have to do a damn thing, but stay black and die, and so I should do the same.

The system sends him to disrupt my meds as I told him, that it's not an accuracy- to life and to lose the inaccuracy of his mindset and welcome the mirror of volume to mirror change.

Freedom

I will never tell our business as to how I am free is a question.

When you have faith, there will come high strength to make it through the toughest times of what you call; I have run out of time because you will not be left alone to raise and carry the burden.

The Unbalanced Gyroscope:

Me:

I needed to balance myself and bring forth- some form of stability as my body was not in orientation and also required a sense of direction. I ran it on red, my body was to ensure me with constant navigation, but inside it was spinning me rapidly into a dizzy and out of place.
I took a much- needed break- from what I love to do, which was -too frail my thoughts on a constant.

What are the thoughts of healing?
Healing is a daily requirement by your mind to stay focus and do what is necessary.
Just like honesty, you have to hold healing in place of its truth to stand and rise at bay to unsuppressed the pain of what you cannot change.

I don't know- where to average myself, so I envision my mind to become educated with the thoughts of knowledge to become one and powerful without fear.
-Learning affirmation to the balance of life-

Freedom won

See balance is between what you can control and hold unto versus what you cannot touch so like your feet to stand still it's the same to water, the waves are at a balance until the wind obstruct it into a disastrous breeze-the effort is to now say to yourself shall I surrender?

If you have chosen to surrender, then your own weakness as emerged from you giving up and falling short on the what-ifs instead of just standing still.

- Things I haven't done in months:
- Watch some good ole Netflix and chill
- Watch television and dwell in some of my favs
- Party in a long time.
- Gone out to dinner-
- This one makes me happy; I haven't drunk a damn thing to get me nice and lose myself.
- Happiness is a madness; many would state yes, unlike me.
- I cannot see myself without not being happy to date.

- Being happy is like a breath of fresh air on my cheeks each day the wind blows, as I look at Rochelle Gapere, seeing how she is living her best life.

I am -placed to where she finds the strength just to give all she can to just win whether or not the allergies are getting to her; she states they are people in the hospital not doing good.

To just live life. Watching how happy people get is a blessing- knowing you are your own power to choose and accept your happiness-without defaults to lend hope a smile in hand.

How does it feel to be me?

Well, if you're with spots and what I call my freckles, your me.

I used to be so insecure by the schupidness of my mindset I refuse to dress in certain things that weren't me-God I would have clothes and don't even put them on.

Freedom won

You can only lose to the thoughts of what you're clinging to; you will know like science there is a solution to every problem, as you, the individual, just need to change it- or just leave what you cannot manage in the end.

Rest in peace, and I tell her my beloved, the truth is I miss you each and every day.
If I had the tools to repair you, I would go in a heartbeat to save your life again.
I love you on my many miles to freedom, and I wanted to tell you I am no longer- enslaved to the bottle of my pain and shame.
I am your mother. I love you, my angel.

I saw this "reading" on a wall today that was "proclaiming" if you genuinely love someone tell them. I loved you, but you left without me explaining, it states heart is often- broken by words left unspoken, but my heart was broken the minutes you stop breathing.
Love to carry pain is, in fact, words to be unspoken of by sadness and broken-hearted lost in betrayal.

" The look you have come to create for my outer exterior- tells me nothing of what my intimate looks like."
It's of no accuracy, and I cannot see my inside. I can only express that pain I bring forth - from within my closet to display and surface pain, so please don't represent any perceptive of me or that you don't know of, which is that you honestly don't know me as a person.
The -Thoughts- of RIGHTEOUSNESS:
Righteousness – is an action to thoughts-
Yes, to become righteous, you must take measures or (ACTION)to become one with oneself.

Righteousness is not just uttering words from your lips- but taking the actions to solidify your movement toward the essence of the spiritual teachings of self-reliance of living and up bringing's of growths toward oneself.
The many distractions of my beauty are my outer layer.
Confusion as to why I don't want an index:
I genuinely don't need any permission to be myself.

Freedom won

I wasn't a grade A student I was just me, as I write more, I see myself —
as I come with incomplete to get to complete- being born was enough,
I told myself that my brilliance lies within me and for me to explore
and excel on, I am for me-
  Hurt, broken, wounded, lost, and "emotionally stress" and obediently
  silent to my pain, I walk out in front of a moving car.

It hit me; I died the last day- to experience life. I was reborn and saved
by a traffic light stop of red on danger. Labels are given to you by
others to settle with. What do you tell yourself?
How do you deal with the negativity at times?
How do -you escape the pressure that they place on you at times?
How do you escape the slavery of your mindset?

Developmental growth where do I place it all?

Then you come up with answers to all of your own questions to answer
them.
(I AM not a failure; I am a person to go through circumstance. I am not
a product of less than, and I am a person with the options to now
choose.
I am not the package to the Product I am a person of my own
rebranding- I have come to emerge yes, I am a product but of change to
my decision to evolve without questions.
Knowing there is absolutely nothing new under the sun, life is just a
repeat to our error, but I am not calling myself lucky I have prayed
really hard to overcome.
Affirmation to my soul:

I stopped to wait for love as it was written for me to find fate. In what
lies ahead of me, it was luv awaiting me.

I needed to tell myself where to find my endless supplies of do over's
and be ok in my case of pain and madness, but oh lord, I have come to
understand the methods of torture and study my own thoughts.
To the ending of a new beginning.

Freedom won

I am not sure what to express as I am letting go of all of me. I told my flesh to stop tempting me into sin because I am done.

As we argued, I was asking myself to know in an army of friends when all battlegrounds of war had approached me, and it never left me alone. My sane came out and proved we can take that walk to rise. So, as I go through each day, I ask of my self-worth to appreciate the values of me like a queen. On the rise to free "myself" and rise daily. As the moon Is my friend, so is the sunlight my friend to glow.

Freedom won

Dear Lord here is my last confession:

Most days, I am in a day as stress and thoughts invest in my head to bleed as I reflect on all my sins and the hurt to suffer.

I am not sure if I am crying, because he is in my head each day and all night long as he approaches my thighs in my sleep.

I Am mostly at a cost to stress as I fester in lust and rage to want to murder, but then there is jail. So here I am confessing all that is in my own head to kill him for wronging me as I grew, so did pain yes more and more.

As I counted all my abusive lovers

I recreated hate for all of them, God I am not sure what I was thinking, but I couldn't be with a saint because I live to recreate harper to kill all my dead cells, kill it all dead yes, I tell you.

As then, satisfaction would caress my "vagina" like sin showing up. To church on Sunday to prey in service, I had been whipped by a tongue to catch the holy of spirit as I shouted Hallie and no lu to yah. I was in a moment of sin to silence as I cry again.

Each day I would get stoned enough to remember God that he would keep me safe, and I would make it back home safe as I receive more of any tongue.

As spiritual as I am most days, I am in remission to think of my madness as to how saliva didn't kill me as I had way too much to swallow each day and night.

I don't know, as I had no loyalty, I was set to schedule another appointment to a weapon and a whipping of tongues.

Lord, most days, I wonder, should I go back to it and let sin have me like a dessert to quench my cat.

Then I am reminded about my journey as I am not a sinner.

As I only watch porn and smoke weed and then release myself than watch and tell God, I am still saved by grace and then repeat the same methods again and tell God the same thing again.

Freedom won

Lord, I am living the worst life known to man as all my exes target me like a check-cashing centre to release cash, God it is not me because I am not dispensing one damn thing.

Most days, I think about him and me, but not for long. That is my ex in my head telling me he still loves me.

As it is wrong to love, I am "sin, "so I cannot be loved by grace because I got buried.

I fell in love with the love of my life at 17 years of age he was my world when all was wrong, as I got one more year older I loved him from afar as I was with another that beat the shit out of me when I wouldn't give myself to him.

He would take all parts of me apart, so I would run to him again to save me as I have nothing but bad experiences into summer, and pain hitting my brain.

I must leave all of my pain and secrets here-

As I am in rehab with my mind, I am not sure if I want to wave myself goodbye at this point.

I haven't seen life in almost 20 years.

Here is where I am off again still in sin, thinking about my past.

Truth after I have all of me and some in telling my story-

I know I left out a lot.

Here is all of me now, I never thought rape would have had me searching for so many things, but it did- like college, my vagina was in a gap year to taking entry like an exam I wanted to find him in what I was searching for.

Kiddie was temp; he was ok nothing too pleasureful.

I am in the error of change because I have become my own truth-in welcoming my own self. I ended my search because love got me naked and making love to my soul.

What I don't know I am trying to figure out as I go through the days of pain and release all of my stress.

Most days, I wondered if I had told my parents of my pain, I wonder if it would have changed me and my outcome as II go through all the hurt.

Freedom won

God knows my heart as sin knows me well to carry me back to all things that hurt and wounded me to stress of no cause.

I have seen many things in my life.
Even the ones that want me to fail my own self, yes, today. As I reflect on a call, I had with my ex.
He told me his heart has never stopped beating for me.
As I cried to no end as to why he hit me, I don't know, as he remembered me. As this broken little girl in pain and needed an escape, we were inseparable, but then he started to beat on me, so I left him for another that would abuse me.

As he asked of me to forgive him, I wanted not to but had to change was upon me, as I cry to grace for saving me.
He had a song playing in my head to reflect on our love triangle as I remember a young man telling me when I break my celibacy come find him then we could date because he is at the peak of where he loves sex wait too much to date me now-
I am not crazy as we both receive a dial to a tone to let go of each other with a message in my head boy bye-
As I reflect on all, I don't need in my life as "bad" baggage, and I let go of all of him never to give him a call-again but then.

I realize I wanted him to hit me as a reminder to feel what my mother felt when that drunk would beat her; how could I want to live that for myself was a question as I now know how foolish I was in the end.

Now I am too much of a woman ever to let that mess happen to me again as forgiveness is my best friend, so is the freedom to grace my lifeline.

Freedom won

Double -Genesis:

The beginning of anything is pain hurt and the ending as they call it a bitter a sweet yes, as I was ready to become a fool again, I invested my time and energy into him to love me once more.

As I am fortuitous to a change and to give myself, I cried about how stupid I was becoming, as I could only reflect on pain and cry nothing but memories of pain.
As a woman, you' are trained to think with the lust of your body and not your soul.
As your heartaches and your chest beat foolishness for him again, who are you kidding?

I was foolish to let him in again with as many times as he had beaten me for what I don't know, as I left him for the second time and when to him for the third time again, I wasn't foolish.

I told myself as I let him beat me again, saying if he didn't beat me as he did before, he didn't love me. Enough or want me enough to hit me again, as this time my eyes were black and blue, as I now get older to want a pair of glasses to wear again like sin it as no glow because I refused to look through them.

I remember I wanted to tell my pain but couldn't fear the judgment of everyone and everything about me being in the open.

Freedom won

Genesis double-take:

So, I spoke in Her about my rape and several takes, but I wasn't sure if many got me as I journaled all of the blue heavens of my own hell to reflect on my own body.

As I prayed, when is the closing of this chapter of "me" at broken going to be over.

As I reran thoughts of pain in that space of mind, I was over the betrayal.

I have heard of love, at first sight, I had that with Oniel as he was the love of my life. In the historic "Era." of changing us with what was a pain as we grew broken, I can a test we both became a toxin to each and how society had us at no worth as we still hurt.

Then I met many to encounter lust for them as I wanted the pain to recreate all my rage as I was again in broken.

As I grew older, I had to ensure to myself I wasn't afraid to talk about my past as I knew Veronica and Lisa had many lovers in the honours of my own body, without asking permission if it was ok. As I genuinely counted up the numbers of my past, I died and returned in a casket to never repeat.

The embodiment of pain is truly painful as I was talking about, genesis here I was walking with my best friend- and this lady out of know where yelled out in the middle of Hoboken, I am trying to sleep, and here you are going with your husband, and disrupting me as I am trying to sleep.

The elements of change are unwarranted; yes, because we don't want change, we want what we have, which is right now, nothing new, nothing different.

Freedom won

I was in the middle of unbalanced when. He calls me as a child in need of a message, so I beg to ask God why are you in my head as I reflect on Genesis.
I have walked in pain as to why I cannot understand the methods of to stand for today and not yesterday.
What am I holding on to is a question as to why?
I am in the genesis of my own mind searching for freedom, and I landed on purpose to rule within one with my mind.

Genesis to whom much is given much is required from as, but the burdens of life won't let you go.
Lord I often pray to have a better way and method to change all things I am in control of, as I pray from within the beginnings of my elements, please aid my hands with discernment to travel into wisdom.

The truth is a beauty mark, and it leaves you in an appropriate balance of memories to create a better vision to see your everlasting.
Everything about loving yourself- is better because it prepared you for your Genesis.
 Everything of natural love will emerge and calm your spirit-
I am a legend, yes, to have carried pain like no other.

My mother never informed me of what labour felt like so, here I was in the middle of giving birth in the delivery room to madness.
I am the process now call Genesis, stating everything of my beginnings of what led me here and kept me broken for many years.

I am not sure how to classify what I felt then, but what I imagine now is everything of change.

I am my mother's child, yes; her prayers have kept me until this day, and she is still praying for me as her child- I am no longer upset about what I couldn't change, but I have gain confidence enough to let go.

All my life, I was treated like a depraved diamond. Rusted and in need of a polish. In her, I talked about all my beginnings and what I did to get here as a person.

Freedom won

One of the most problematic "things" to ever had worked out through and within my own head, what all people did to me as a person overall.

I was wondering if I was suffering from "post-traumatic" stress disorder.
The thoughts of PTSD as my burden were a bit much, so as I drowned in pain, I would wake up thinking that I kill me each night.

I now understand that I gave them energy to carry-to think that they had any control over me.
I was in this bottle call all of my sin surrounded by rage and pain and hate. To always recreate hate, today, I asked a question, and I got an answer to disrupt my soul because, like others, she still viewed me as not good enough.

The error of corrections is to judge as always.
One of the many things of her is raw after I wrote this challenging piece. I got several questions on the many levels of why I stated I don't want to get married.

As I was in a conversation with a young lady, she was promoting and quoting the bible to me as I reflect on Genesis.

Again, I was curious because she dears to educate me, so I wanted to ask her how ole is Adam and Eve, and if all the biblical teachings are to any accuracy, so she debated my head to stress the cause of unknown to known facts.

The bible to me is taken out of context yes-
The conversation got more interesting as she dears herself again-to ask me why I stated I am a Goddess, so I reply with an answer to the state of I am a God in my own right to feel and view what flows through me my self.
As she judges me in her head as she calls herself a woman of God, her view to me serves no benefits to my soul because here "she" was now engaged in a conversation to call another human ugly why others stated she is hard to look at-

Freedom won

Then prophesy, they loved God when they were judging is creation.
As she reads or flashes through the pages of her raw burden, all things
approach her thoughts as she gave me back my device and stated good
luck and all the success.

As her "mind" state reflects in my rare view, I noted she wasn't pleased
that I could evolve to consciousness; yes, she was thinking in her head a
gyal like "shi" still views her love for God.

It is Funny how Genesis is like having a conversation with your Massa.
He is asking you; nigga did you draw up the thesis I asked you for, as in
if he is doing you a favour after having you in slavery, so like the
beginning, you become curious as to why he as so much power over
YOU?

I am the beginning to no end, as my thoughts rise like I buried ashes.
I am the ground not to be walked upon. But fly as my dust gathered
away like a bird flying in the air. As the heavens of my head are attached
to my body.
I am still a Goddess in search of which garden did my molestation got
started in. As to why he betrayed me, and how old was I?

The wings of my life is a pain-filled with secrets to relate and grieve to
my thighs.
I am looking at him, my heavenly father. The inner son of man and soul
of a woman not human to like because I have a fault, I am the alpha to
the genesis and gone like a revelation, was curious then and foolish but
why to ask now the question was this my journey within pain?

The origin of me is in the beginning to an end starting from the middle
into reverse was thought to clutch as I am wondering if I was going to
pray to myself or God, then I realize I would be praying to the inside of
my self because he lives in me.
So as the sun was about to set. I rinsed my face and covered my head
and kneel to the methods of my mind as I yarn in a loud to tell.
I was still in a "yern" of my yearning.

Freedom won

As I was receiving to my needs of the same methods. To want as I cry to learn about what I missed in the genesis of my garden to pain.
As the womb of my own body is obsolete, I am in the middle to understand yes. I am outdated and no longer able to produce so that I won't be travelling to my destination but my empty barrel to my outmoded body.

Opening up was the hardest:
I wanted to have the craziest convo to self as to why I hate and luv being vulnerable
When you view peace as the source to embody the elements of grace and inner being to exist, you have grown the elevations of your mind. Letting go of many in the elements of change.
I genuinely don't know "where" my pain stops, but I know where it got started, as I have learned never to run into people because they can be great pretenders of the world, and everything is GAME for them.
The methods of many "is" convenience and what you can do for them as it is the methods of always wanting. To be in the know of what is going on with and nothing about them.

The thoughts of many are that they love me, which is all lies as I stress my depression.

 I saw not one; as I re-evaluate my friendships with many, I am in a better place, and I see that they were never for me.
I have learnt that "many" person thinks to themselves if they don't support your vision or your achievements in life that you won't be successful and excel.

As I had to learn that many were more my enemy than a friend and my users, I got tired and push them out like a delivery to give birth to a baby.
I left them in the delivery door like a depraved placenta that I wasn't going to eat, as I learnt that God will equip you with total strangers that will hold your hands and give you better support than they will ever give to you.

Freedom won

Memories and pain:

As a child, your taught to do your best because there is always someone watching and waiting to notice, so for years, I struggled with the same methods as to why no one sees my pain.

As you have read me her pain, you will know what I feel as to madness of rage.

I remember being young and sharing a personal secret with a young man about what I when through with this guy and how he had hurt me.

Today is a beautiful day I am alone with my thoughts as I am freeing myself from bondage and pain.

I looked up to glare at a message sent to me from my precious timeline stating in my head not everyone deserves access to you nor your energy, so it's required for you to protect your spirit from what doesn't give you purpose.

So, as I am in the elements of my mind, I will continue to love me beyond today and tomorrow to gain.

I will breathe my inner love until my lungs give out on me. I will love me until my own heart stops beating, that intimate love of beloved.

As I sit and carry my inner love. I know now never to entertain what doesn't give me energy.

As it is written, fake people have an image to maintain, and because my heart is authentic, I give not too shyt of their views on me because I AM real to my soul and have nothing to maintain but continue to uphold quality.

The thoughts of breaking up with love and waking up in a life of beloved are the best feeling in the entire world.

Honestly, knowing the elements of all my solutions to any problems that may arise is my blessing to rise.

I am currently in my current state, as I will soon reflect on my former state.

Every problem can be fixed.

So as long as I am willing to access all things, I can change it or leave them in the same place to continue hurting me. I gave to acceptance, so I decide to change, and no longer offer 'change.

Freedom won

Because I am in the error of not believing in luck or the magical nonsense, however, I believe in God's grace and mercy and all his many blessings.
The thoughts as to why I feel alone in the world is a bother to my methods of madness.

The stress of pain keeps me in that bottle. As to the loneliness, I feel from not being loved by her my own.

I am not sure if it's my insecurities or just the pain of not having her to protect me. As I am in constant wonder of my shame, the cries continue as I eat myself away.
I am now up to a hundred and fifty pounds from eating myself away
As to why I eat myself away is of no structural balance but a   hurting, I feel so I just do it.

My rage is so bitter about revealing my hate for him I feared that I shouldn't have forgiven him for raping me nor he for abusing me.

As to why I was in a different level or element with the thinkings that he didn't mean to hurt me was a lie to my soul.
I felt a release, yes, to find therapy in healing from them. But I forgot to measure what would surface in me rage hate and tormentation of him taking me into his bed.
I honestly didn't think of the psychological damage of it until I realize my innocence was -broken at ages 12 to 19 years of age.
I knew nothing of my body other than rape created a high for me and that I needed to feel the pleasure of what he left me with, whether it was a tongue or the thoughts of him raping me or recreating it. I was always looking for that feeling to feel sane.

The fight.

I cannot memorize what I haven't learnt, and I cannot "learn" what I haven't "memorized" of anything in reverse is as I don't know what being in your arms feels like. As I can only imagine your hugs and soft touch, I don't remember learning from you. This is love.

Freedom won

Fear:
Countless times I was, becoming like you.
I lost my innocence to many things as I hurt, I fear what as well can I
do but other than fight with you was a method to stay.

I fought with my mother the other day only to express what I was
feeling, but I never stopped and valued her pain her hurt what her
mother did to her leaving her to grow up rough without a home.
As I continue to listen, I view things differently because I know she is
hurting and is in pain to wonder how her mother could be so
inhumane.

The challenges she is facing is far greater than my pain as she had never
stopped to receive any treatments of therapy nor closure to close out
what "she" was carrying on the inside of her I honestly don't know how
she feels at the end of all pain to take.
The thoughts of how I could even be upset with my mother are my
blank.
As the thoughts of all the love she gave to me is a plus-
I now understand that my mother loves me effortlessly- and she had
made a tremendous sacrifice to carry me. I salute her.
Why am I not sure as of today's date?

I asked the question a few days ago why I wrote. Myself in those
methods to express raw. As I had no answer other than I was tired of
living in the shadows of my rape-
As I was afraid to answer any questions, I also feared to talk about how
people were going to treat me as a person and what I worried as I
walked into a room filled with everyone asking me questions.
The hardest thing for me was to sit and talk about my pain and all the
challenges.
Love is the death of duty, and the reverse of function is death to
sacrifice one's self-giving yourself as a duty serves to a cause.
I saw a mirror today, yelling at me as to why I had just gone through
the methods of fighting with my mother for the many reasons that she
didn't understand my pain.

Freedom won

It was Friday before Sunday as she would learn how I genuinely feel about suffering and the hurt I was enduring, in my head of madness, as she asked the question if I was mentally unstable and going crazy.

How much I wanted to cry as I yelled at her loudly with bitterness and hurt in disbelief as to why I think she must genuinely hate me to believe it's ok to understand my pain.
It's the 12th of May as the 10th of May was a pain I was reflecting on our pain.

I was honestly so broken as I don't celebrate the methods of Mother's Day. I had to text my brother to extend a Mother's Day shout out to my queen as I was in tears.

As God was upon me, I couldn't command my release to stop hurting as I continue to cry. There was no joy in me left only tears.
The wind of God had me as the breeze had me at a realization to stand and continue to cry to God as to why I am still in pain.
I wasn't thinking straight as I continued to drink.
My vodka to no reverse and drunk was approaching me.

As I ran to cover up my act of me, before Eric got up upstairs, I brush away my teeth and engage myself to make a mint as I pray he wouldn't notice I was drunk out of my mind.

At this point, I was asking God to shield me from all my pain and help me free my spirit into freedom.
My body was selfish to STAND, so as I couldn't breathe light, I burst out to him take me to the hospital, I need help before I kill myself, please.

As he turned around, I was moments away from taking my last breath as he yelled out, I am not raising three babies by myself you self-fish phuck, this is not about you what about them, what you want me to tell them that you kill yourself?
Well, I am not doing that shyt so put that damn knife down I am getting dressed so please let's go for a drive as he held on to my hands

Freedom won

he said nothing but the words of please breathe as he asked me if he was talking to Veronica or Lisa because he couldn't live without either of us.

He was driving, and all I could see was the tears running from his own eyes as is voice got softer to why I would want to end my own life.

My external rooting was dying in pain, as I carried out the layers of madness I was still hurting in my pain.
The invalidation of the methods of torture was haunting—me like a ghost -as I look up and validate my life to live or die.

As I was thinking about my purpose to live my best life, I was gaining a new sense of love for myself.
Self-love is the most excellent method of loving yourself from within as I had to learn the techniques of change again.
Expressive was my method of thought to think and breathe out loud-as I needed to process that if I wasn't active, my tears were going to kill me.

Along with the fears of not understanding my self-
I used to express all my rage into a bottle now here I was with nothing.
I was expressing my own heart to make a decision. To free my self and my own heart to break free from my own reality.
Making my own decisions was a must as I didn't care about the nonsense of life.
The methods to think about my madness to date hate is a pain as I cry tears.

- Remembering him nailing my vagina how he could enter me was a question-

I don't know what to make of things because on this journey of truth, and you. Learn who is indeed your friend.

I. I learn to stop myself from the emotional side of my outer layer to care who wants to share my views and pain because, honestly, I don't think you were ever going to support me.

As I was starting to BE in a "good" place, I receive hurt.

Freedom won

I sit most days in a corner with my pain, trying to focus on the methods of how-to mother my heart to take the disappointment of humans.

Then I receive a text to show me my son's report card, its states oh Rayden is an excellent reader, but indiscipline my takes is that what can you say to a child that the system labels as having ADHD-
-Affirmation to excel and change with grace I bid.
-Detailed to express my inner thoughts
- H hope to gain and never lose.
-Determinedly challenging myself –
Please stop labelling me and calling me outside of my name.

R .A.Y.D.E.N
- ✓ Reasons to be- reminded
- ✓ Acquired not slow, he is expressing miss lady you are clearly stating he is a good reader.
- ✓ Yelling to be accepted
- ✓ Defined and underestimated by society's methods of my abilities as a human, please.
- ✓ Education is my level to level up to your paste, but you don't know what I no.
- ✓ Nobel to change -

For the next time, they make it seem like your nonexistent to feel and hurt.
I would love for you to check my levels and not define me on the levels of ADHD.
  Hearing my son's cries hurt me so severely as I pretend to be influential; I am as "numb" as he is to understand pain.

- ▪ Attentive to comprehend they don't want to aid me to be progressive
- ▪ Understanding the methods to observe the "methods" put in place to drug me up is what next right?
- ▪ Talented you cannot see as I learn many languages
- ▪ Intelligent I pose great intellect to relate
- ▪ The smart lady I am self-taught leaves me alone.
- ▪ Televised – evolving beyond what you're thinking of me, yes.

Freedom won

- Informative pressing inward to knowledge
- Changing the future watch and see how I will exceed.

Then here comes society that thinks less of your child.

As if you can't escape the methods of becoming, as I continue on my path of finding most days, I still wonder why I wrote her as well.

I got pregnant with my son after a painful miscarriage; now, here I am trying to understand what did I do wrong. But then again. I am truly blessed to understand the growth of myself as a woman and a mother on a whole.

Madness.

The feelings to gain wins-
Love will always win:
Love is the center to her as he is the middle of her that always wins her.
Love is to the making of essence that will win as he is telling me, letting go is hard, and being free is beautiful as he shows me free to love again.
The self-care to reflect on all things to benefit- thinking about the last man standing as madness and look you in the eyes to give yourself to him before the end of death arise at the front room.

The day of pain reflects us all in the end:
can you imagine your virgin breast becomes "unvirgin" and your welcome to the sexual feelings of a feel, but you get entered as you never believed giving yourself to no one, but here comes him, and he took all of you?
I have come to appreciate my thoughts:
The purpose is again to confirm the self-embodiment of self-love-
Getting to know your writes as luv become one with you in that 7 seconds you will take to drain your strength, give life a turnaround into hope to love oneself to free the mind of thoughts that only you can change from every negative into a positive and see the light.

- The same levels of thinking create as well, so if you create only the negative, how can you start to receive anything positive.
- Energy is gifted and birth by self and thoughts, so in reverse, you will come to create your problems.

Freedom won

Remember that greatness of powers comes with high strength of responsibilities- a person must genuinely meet one's demands with benefits to receive love for oneself and aid the rights to live. The wheel will power to present growth in the inner you.

As I sat in on the walls of my memories, I cry to the heavens to live above grace and live above change —

I am mentally aware of all my changes to give self-love and bring self-methods to my honour.

As I remember, pain all over as to why. I wrote her was to bring much-needed awareness to abuse and torture, I was approaching 15 years of age when all my pain got started as I have come to understand the methods of people, I believe in life over pain as I live on the lengths of hope I gain my freedom to breathe.

- The balance awaits you to exercise all your writes to the right, yes.
- Never allow yourself to be a tool for another man's exercise; it's a state of you being "an" equipment to ride for his joy and pleasures while he releases, he laughs at you.
- You must learn to await your balance to change and progress in life.
- It's imperative how you speak, things into the path of existence, yes.

In the middle of RAW, I remember stating honour is a privilege given, but still, never give recognition to what 'doesn't provide you with reputation.

The methods of leaning on self to achieve are accurate because only your true self can disappoint oneself in the end toward growth.

- Being alone with your thoughts is a madness; yes, as you can recreate them into positives, stop the viewing of all things negative on your journey.
- Humility, grace, and trust cometh come from the inner you, to reconnect.
- Logically I bring my pain to a fourth front to have a feeling.

Freedom won

- Biologically I gave it wings of emotions to let pain think it can fly like it has (wings).
- Mental madness is a thought left to go rotten and like a flower; it requires more and more water.

The benefits of my personal -problems are not yours to receive because you have no loyalty to my pain, only your views. To opinionate your just too close in the passing of which you cannot apply. The base of this is to state I am my thoughts as I can only xpress to you, while you will still or may not have a clue to help me deal with pain.

Many "beg" to differ has to pain is to reflect I do need your thoughts to relate yes.
As I may need treatment, you only view your benefits as my therapist to sit and collect the information given because the sadness is only words to you to give your takes on and think I should settle with

- It's written what a hand fully knows thousands will become privy to as it means to give away as opinions on your views as you talk about my problems.

I needed to understand many whys and get answers to questions I have. My mother is very much sad on the inside of her walls. To reflect on beloved as she too has questions as to why her mother didn't love her and gave her away to suffer nothing but pain.

As I come to learn about my body, I became sexless to celibacy again to understand why he entered me to damage my interior when I can't afford to fix my thighs to the rape of pain.

At 16, I was disobedient and needed nothing to bring me to hope to gain access to do better and aim for me because I was- broken by pain. As the thunder roll on many days of pain, the falling of the raindrops becomes more massive, and the wind of pain captured me again.

The methods of pain continued as I gave birth to another illness.

Freedom won

The first day he hit me, I was foolish to think I was like my mother, not understanding my pain.

--

--

I ran "to" many things.

My poor mother did her best, but I couldn't tell her of my pain as I didn't care to reflect nor tell.

I believe I played house to understand the whys of how he could enter me and left me rotten.

As I cry many nights, nothing was coming to save me, did the church of man fails me yes absolutely because they did nothing to bring awareness to pain nor depression of youth in pain.

The thoughts of people were to label me like a slut going around, looking back and passing those ladies that states to me I wouldn't have become anything in life nor achieve, I don't even care to wonder.

Gather yourself to think and evolve on your balance.
I walk my path to choose and excel, now here comes the grace to enhance.

All my life, I understood nothing about my own body- I only knew to want the feelings of pain again and again.
I have come to appreciate my body in my thirties as I was willing to give away one of my liver. I realized and was -informed I only have one can you believe this, me thinking that I was a double person standing

Freedom won

with four kidneys and two liver and multiple heartbeats to beat sound I 'wasn't myself again.

As I have come to dishonour of the things of vanity and appreciation of the elements of life and nature, I found love to gain experience.

Affirmation to state yes, we need things, but what is money? When God is aiding me to attract all things in the life of growth and development to welcome change to gain access.

-I now have love and all the amazing characteristics of experience to give me joy.

I amazingly breathe the opportunities of life as I shame the devil and tell my truth to heal as I now breathe easily.

The protection of my energy is necessary to gain:

Life is the most expensive thing to have because we cannot truly afford it as we take for granted what others want.

It's only to say no to others, and cancel the devils stand to see you fail, never commit to what doesn't give you joy.

I can change my thoughts, but my mind, I will always be made up to stand for its justice.

Learning that if you continue to dwell, you will never move to past the pain if you're still residing in the past of pain by living in it, you heal when you change, and evolve and start living in the presence of things to gain balance.

We need to learn that life is short, so our focus is to concern it with living until we have ended -is- a plus-

Enjoy laughter and love because beliefs cannot be- broken unless you let; it loses its essence and brings emotions on the outside of you to lust.

Peace of mind:

The order requires and needs an assistant to stay.

You don't have to be absent because the things of life will always be present to (fuel) hurt and pain.

Conflict; and difficulties look for the problem, and it doesn't seem to anyone for making a difference.

The powers of knowledge are to educate oneself as freedom teaches you to evolve.

I am not sure to the pure, but I am worthy of feeling.

Freedom won

As I am not perfect, I learn to avoid pain.
The thoughts of "unbreakable" love will always and forever connect us.
The powers of pain have hurt the mind of us as one is conjoined as one
let me breathe -is never an option.

Love will break as it will heal.
The thoughts of suffocation:
 As I have come to rise, I breathe a breath to suppose daily thinking
about so many things, as I shared a cruel pain with my poor mother, as
to this point, I am not sure if its betrayals, blame, or resentments
carrying its way to me.

The human heart in me wants to heal, but my pain stems from a place
of pain, I put your needs first yes, I would give you the first, but I don't
know where the void is.
That was me in a state of madness as to why you betray me?
I have been wanting to tell you something but will carry it to fire as I
know you know we don't have to ever speak on it because I am passing
it.

Freedom won

———————————————————————
———————————————————————
———————————————————————

The stressful date is my phone:

I have done a lot of things in the reverse of life because I didn't want to talk about my pain.

So as a mother, your training thoughts are way different as an aunt; your view is different, yes, so on March 27th of this year, I didn't celebrate my birthday as usual because I didn't care about the month nor date, it was making.

As I receive a call on the 28th into the 29th, I knew I had failed as a mother to my niece, as I heard my sister express to me my niece stated she wanted to die.

As to why I didn't ask, but then the topic changed to her letting me know my niece tried to kill herself again, my heart dropped as to why I couldn't breathe my entire mind when will my soul turning my body into ashes back again, I am to the soil.

She was depressed about life, and what the peers of her age group were doing to her reality to escape was to un-exist from living, in purpose. The experiences of my pain were -transferred because I knew where she was in terms of losing herself to illness.

I had to prepare myself to talk to my niece, as she was my actual first love, I knew what not to say, but I needed to express.
As I told her beloved is a precious gift, and she needed to love everything on the inside of her.

I was trying to help her make sense of her void as I heal from my pain. I could relate to her shock because I tried killing myself. As well- God knowing the madness and the pain going through her broken little heart, what was I going to do to heal her my soul assembled into dust as I planned to enter her body to show her beloved as I couldn't touch her face in the physical but in spirit.

———————————————————————

Freedom won

I gave her the courage to breathe; as I cry with her, I knew we would get through the rain just not today.

As I still reflect, I blame what was created in our household, as I ask the question, was there any love? As I wasn't- showered with hugs nor kisses, and I had so much driven me into insane, I drank another bottle of cough syrup as to why she was in pain, as I wonder, did someone hurt her?

As I view my madness, I wondered about my girls, how could I not see her pain, my poor baby.

The methods to think something or someone was bewitching you was madness to suffer because nothing made any sense, as I confidently wrote my truth on the walls of madness. I can't breathe again.

The thought of stress captured me at the turn of suffocation.

I found myself again, thinking I needed the facade of my madness to create what wasn't there for many to see, but I knew I was living in pain to relate to myself each day.

March 18th, 2019

I was here in the middle of my mind as it was about 10 seconds ahead of me, as I call my mother to express my stress of my soul rapidly. I was telling her I was pleading to myself to pledge allegiance to date and expire the madness of my pain.

1. I pledge to be at the utmost of my truth, between me and sin.
2. I pledge to liberate my shame from rotten to fresh and scented free of a whore.
3. I pledge to stop my drinking/ addiction to madness.

---

4. Make the necessary decisions to take on my meds
5. Freedom to freely welcome growth.
6. I have committed myself not ever to drink- nor abuse alcohol
7. I am freeing myself from being addicted to the tongue of a woman or man.

Freedom won

_____
_____
_____
_____

I declare myself:

Alecia Smith

On today's- date, I PROMISE to stop the numbering of myself and start to hold myself accountable and to renounce the drinking of poison to bear fate and listen to the teachings of the word of the "Infinite" without any mental reservation. I am a person with problems yes acknowledgment is necessary if I don't change in time the bottle will kill me, so yes, I solemnly swear to immediately no longer drink-

I will only serve you and not my sins. In the purpose of circumvention, I will maintain as required blessings on a daily I will prey to pray.

I am under the understanding of faith and prayer to daily, as I bound both my visible and invisible- mind to only you, as the sea to water runs, I will run to only you lord.
I will prey and pray unto the responsibilities of making the impossible possible because I am within you, and you're with me, so I shall bid all things through you cometh and endure.

"The ashes that centred "centered" me from the flames of a dragon's mouth burn me into unrecognizable- as the phoenix recreate me, I am arising in water."

The day of my madness is unfiltered to unfit- I got a new upgraded camera to take my picture as I look at Denial and take a chance on freedom, I welcome the-date to date of noise, and I heard the voice of my mother yelling, why? The covering of your beauty. As I tell her of

Freedom won

my "Hindrance" into distraction, and the attraction of the look at sin, she replied with I now understand your methods to be unseen.

===
=======================

------- God is love, and his luv, covers a multitude of my sins -and your sins, so let the forgiveness- reign in royalty to honour his name to be lifted -up in the deliverance of what you cannot control or take with you in the end.

"I have come to outline my bullet points to my madness- please me as I erase myself to sane, she was asking God to cash her out, God ask why I was still standing, I told him I was awaiting my receipt."

The truth about me is in a blank space awaiting me to fill her up completely — to incompletely.

I am a servant of sin born in sin, so why do I need redemption?
I honestly don't know, as I age with the disease of madness- I don't stress seeing the end I know it's coming.

I have come to be - the applicant, to apply for my job to madness, the unknowingly- truth about my application is that I don't know what I am signing off on other than depression is in my presence.

I hate the food of nature to the pain that releases the toxins to my madness.

So, I went to the store of cleansing- to tell the shop of keepers that I need a washout.
He was looking at me like what can I help you with as I reply again, letting him know a volcano is approaching my butt of disturbing shyt in his midst if he wants to stand, I will apply a splash of brown to glory on him.

Freedom won

Be the best to become the better version of your soul.
Thrive for your worth to gain values, don't ask for appreciation from what don't give you inner peace and satisfaction to your growth of internal peace of mind.

I am getting myself together to listen to my heart as I hear the sound of pain, emerged from my darkest days- II am near to gold and silver as I reflect on the grass on grassing on grassing green to yellow in my heart the pain is still right there.
So, I woke up my soul, who is too ole to remember yesterday because she is in today and lost to next month while remaining in this month.

Speak:
The utterance to deliver greatness is to excel talent; it is from the birth of creation. Everything on the inside of you, no one can take away your heart unless you serve it up to them on a platter, to give your rights away to choose.
Consciousness is the formation of righteousness- of the mind to exhale greatness. So I started to breathe light I wanted to shine from within.
I am here today because I let my own heart to a miracle of inner peace.

===
===============================

The thoughts to failing were measured as optional because I have crossed all those barriers already.
To my then shame, so I held on to me like glue, and I shake off the fear.
I smiled into me to rebuild hope because I am a God to the Goddess-because he exists through me and within me.

I breathe life, so I am living."
 Knowingly -knowing my strengths of who I am. To him and who I shall serve myself.
Through him over and again in time. To be reborn into a soul that was once lost to the mind of shame.

Freedom won

I have met many I have spoken to many, with fakes smiles and the look of I got you is nothing short of I can't wait until she stops talking and gets out of my face.

--

First, look

It was our first ultrasound of your heart beating inside of me; then I later saw your ten toes; you're my first always and forever. I sew my heart next to yours, so you're still beating in me we are one and never apart, us is forever your umbilical cord is my- stem the same way my universe to feud lite of the day you're my first look at the light. Reannie, you're always my good luck charm. You are never away from me, but right beside me. As I reflect on your hands touching me, I am at peace, smiling next to you.

==
==============================

Legacy:

My babies are my everything,

Motto:

Whatever writing is or isn't, I love it, because I am not averaging my thoughts.

I let it become an avid of my air to breathe words and sense to feel and identify me A -Assertive, L-Life E-Empowering, C-Committed I-Indigenous, - A-Assurance.
Alecia.

Grandmother:

Dedication to my grandmother,
I dreamt of you, and you came to me, I have a piece of your soul inside of me deeming me to do good, your smiles reflect me every day.

Freedom won

I look at you in my dad to see what your heart looks like, and you have kept me safe and sane, sending me back in thoughts.

I quoted you in my head when I am at a low, to see life to hold on to your eternal to my grace as I sing change me oh God and make me more like you. Sip in everlasting Aunty John.

I know I have failed at assembling our family's "reunion," but I will let it happen.

In Canada, I was on your grave to scent your feelings as you hug my pain to a let go, I kneeled to you to welcome apart of you to me, so I am grateful.

Freedom won

_____

_____

_____

Promises

I have watched the world promised to me and received nothing but
use instead and lies to digest, baring the thoughts to a corrupt
digestive system that couldn't do anything to deliver me.

Then cometh back again all the bullshit, I started to only listen to
myself and doing for me. I became now not settling for foolishness; I
see the pretender to give you pain.
They were never happy for you; only the lies adjusted to keep you
oppress and at a standstill.

_____

"Being educated is everything and nothing at the same time; to deliver
a draft with typos and error doesn't mean your slow."

It means you are trying to excel, but to have someone take that idea
and turn it into something and turn it around and say, don't worry,
you're in great hands.

I got you I feel your pain and never showed up when your ready is a
slap in the face, so what do you do is a question I had for myself.

So, I got up, and I ran to one thing that kept me sane to the writing
of my pain, I was fixing everything for- myself, I did the work as a jail
sentence I serve my mind to enlightening my brain to spark. The
greatness I produce is from all within me."

_____

Freedom won

The day I stop letting your opinion of me be of relevancy, I became myself.
I will never entertain your views of me because they don't matter, you are not my edges, so you don't need any control to hold me together I have me.

The next time you see me, keep all your statements for your testimony because I have already testified my pain, and I didn't see you when I was crying.
The thoughts to everyone are that they know me, the truth is you don't, I have never asked of you, you have never come running to save me from my beatings nor madness.

As I close my door to the ones that have never cared for me nor valued my pain, I close my door to the thoughts of shame to let go like bad baggage.
I am pleased to access my soul to remain at you will always be my forever; you will always be mine.

I have to place my madness at historical to historical the walk it took to get here wasn't easy, but I am here for the internal lesson of my mind and brain developing more-wisdom.

Freedom won

"MAD"

Mind awakens & developed.
Is the truth to trash your heart, and find your mind that feeds your
soul to attribute your attitude" gain" with value and "thrives" to do I
am at 80%

The picture to my context, I "Reflect" my look:
"With the thoughts of not making up my truth, I have been commonly
called mad and peculiar associated with sickness, of I, need help, with
their laughter to deem me at my uncertainties."
I was at work with a seven to reflect all my ego's and identify them to
my mode Monday to Sunday. I was Rebecca, and a half-day I was
Alecia, Lisa Becky, Maria, Veronica Victoria.

I was packing to mail to myself daily some days I FedEx myself, and
most days I UPS, and USPS myself.

I deal with Veronica crying and Lisa drunkenness and Becky smoking
pot; I deal with Rebecca's blondeness, and yes, the Maria that whores
through my mind daily, I suppress everyone when Alecia comes alive
because she is the smartness of us all.

I have my Certificate to proof unproved to myself was a conversation
Lisa was having with Alecia- she was telling me. Never express her
because I wasn't there to expedite her thoughts in sensing her pain to
rape, I wasn't there I said to her when it happens to all of us?
Why did you create all of us? To hide my pain and shame, so I didn't
even have to deal with this pain?
I place my thoughts to paper with passion, and I put me in a race to
never disgrace myself and to ensure my ancestors know I remember
them and will always page homage.
March 16th, I am busy becoming better as a statement to myself.
  Comments to her:
  My self-evaluation is today.

Freedom won

Me: I am a full-sentence point-blank and PERIOD mad.
I am a complete case looking to find my serial number, as I am sitting
and writing my pain.
As we discuss, I am angry to fake smile at where you will know to kiss
my A my shrink is searching for me instead of me searching for her.

Freedom won

TO MYSELF:
I am still on March the 15th of another Friday with hopes of fake sunshine. The weather that relates to me I am sick kinda- weather.
I am knowledgeable to inhabitants, and I am wisdom to inherit, now my qualifications are set at deeming- mad as I express my love life and the 14 years of damage sin.

Who am I today is so different from last night, I am not Rebecca showing off my teeth's, and selling my breast, I am breathing?
I was running to him to access me. He told me the main woman in his life needed him, so goodnight.

I asked if I was the third wheel because he was in love with another.
As if I should give two shyts about her.
So, Alecia came out and was disciplining, Rebecca to leave that man alone, he doesn't want you only the idea of you.
Luv, I disagreed with forever as he calls me less and less, and he distances himself from me. I was never going to luv again.
I don't know her, so I guess she is lucky because I am insane to him and depths to luv him.
As I dream of accessing her so we can share him because killing her would be a crime, with a sentence.

I was going to serve so she can have in on the days I don't want him like a custody battle, we have our own time for takes, I will phuck him on set to last Monday into noon.
As I watch him rinse his cock to service you at 1:00p.m., don't worry, my essence is flavoured to the taste of pineapple.
We are now even no bad blood, just a shortage of man to give cock, so I care.

Freedom won

I was his target and a masterpiece in progress, and I am like the insurance to progressive my vagina, the medium to well done up he is staying with me and will soon leave her.

The thoughts, to high performance. High definition, high speed. Knowing with speed, I am a lightening level; I was placed at an exceptional solution today. I wasn't going mad.
I was running on the strength of yesterday, in wanting to alleviate my madness, I was reducing it on a scale.
The poverty of my mind is a sad case to a file, locked away in a cabinet, Alecia is a pain not of thoughts to account but poison to suffer fuse to blow as sin is to curse.

Reasoning thoughts, to asking myself, why should I or why do I even work so hard?
I am cleaning my hurt into clean, but this broom is the purpose of telling me to stop sweeping and mob my pain instead, because the dust will still be there, so I should wipe it away.
So here I am, wiping. All of me, a way to new, and I get myself to say hello Alecia.
Today I was clean to rinse her as I burn Lisa with grease to shine.

March 16th
I am still in March only in a different element to pain as I was assisting a customer my bad shoulder when to give out on me why I don't know.
As the talks are all about the day of events and half of America is missing.
To attend the long walk to freedom.
I was attending to my dislocated shoulder; the pain was excruciating to oppose I was cussing in my head as to why this shit happened already last month and again this month.

Freedom won

Love:
Deemed treasured.

I have fallen way too deep into you has your breaking me open as I will oddly release myself on to you due to the timing of a sacred kiss.
I am the first, third, and second to danger as I was once in love with not being shown enough love.

I cannot cry for what wasn't- given unto me as a person. I wasn't asking for the lies of love. But it was looking to take advantage of me, so as each late-night sleep to a cry. I am okay and at peace without Love.

She is not only just sinning her in the elements of searching for Alecia her self to find beloved and light of day again.

I am lost at sea now to reflect danger on my mind, please don't come to me until I am truly ready to feel still beloved.
As you were the devil in me daring me to kill me, my self, I am still in October to not pick up my results from death by Sheldon as he was the last to access me on a drunken Saturday night.

Today is November 7th, the day of my sister's birthday, as I have cometh to unblock her. I genuinely wish I liveth to see life-like her un innocent and burden-free from secrets.
Samson did nothing to Delilah has per the bible but look at the murderous ways of her lips of lies that broke that man.

Delilah is the same as Veronica. The devil to my vagina tainted from a long day of not being washed and cured of piss and scented odour.

I honestly don't think my vagina loves me as it recaps on Veronica hunting again, can your vagina entrap you and coaxed to revealing too many, you're a drunk and a sex addict to slut your thighs still for the tongues of men.

Freedom won

My vagina took advantage of me and stole my confidence to betray me daily; I name her my enemy, to murder.
She pretends to be my strength, but God, who is in heaven, knows she is a symbol of madness.

As I dread the suicide of it, I am afraid it will come back to haunt me. As I am left alone to carry pain like fresh almonds growing, and the breeze of milk whistling from the thoughts of me thinking.

I wished I was still a baby on my mother's breast again. I am polished to unpolished as the pain grows more on me. I now knew the death of me planning to end me as ended me without planning as I have killed me by the hands of Veronica.

As I end me in pieces of what is my peace of mind being- shattered, I am free.
As I am at beloved to discover freedom, I have cometh to realize my demons were also protecting me from pain to shield my then and current broken state of madness.

Freedom won

TO BE CONTINUED.

If I could change my pain from the burden, I would find my age has a newborn baby again. Free from worries and only have my cries and feeding time, yes.

Now that I am freed from my self and the renovations of reconstructing. My patterns of writing to fit me and readapt myself to a read are now completed. Lord, I beg for no mercy still, yet I do fear the judgments of men and timing. So I have poured myself a drink to reign in 2020.

There is no purple in life other than the streaks of the rainbow. Life is as black and white as we know it.

The moon is no bluer than the fogs than glow half white. Like the stars in the sky, aid us to light and bloom a flower; sometimes, it is best to leave many things dead.
"I bodied death. I just didn't see the sins coming to take me home."
I am no shame in need of an umbrella because I can not escape the rain as it is pouring the drips is a sign to seal my ashes. I am forever and will forever be as the freckles on my skin is permanent, so is death.

We use many things, just not words, as they are two powerful to reflect on the shames we carry.

I am often --told to think in silence and breathe in that same temperament.
As I am not a fox in the wild, I have found a lion to say to me roar.
Awaken to your eyes, and we ignite purpose to love, breathe and fear not will be.

Freedom won

"The light is as bright as a kiss from the sun. Love as no colour. My heart is "universal. "As I am continuous, I fear nothing because I cannot escape meant to be my death."

"I am my own as a shadow; it is all of me in twos and ones the shell is my body, and my spirit is my thoughts. I cannot purchase either because my vessel sits to rot, and my shadow travels without me most days."

Freedom won

Alecia Smith
Da writer
Her Raw Burden Vol#2
Da end of growth starts at the beginning of volume three.

Freedom won

Freedom won